DUROC

DUROC

by

SIMON W. PAIN

www.Penmorepress.com

DUROC
By Simon W. Pain
Copyright © 2024.Simon Pain

All rights reserved. No part of this book may be used or reproduced by any means without the written permission of the publisher except in the case of brief quotation embodied in critical articles and reviews.

ISBN-13: 978-1-957851-36-5(Paperback)
ISBN-13: 978-1-957851-35-8(e-book)

BISAC Subject Headings:
DRA000000DRAMA/ General
FIC001000 FICTION/Action
FIC031000 FICTION/Thrillers

Editor: Lauren McElroy

Cover Design:
EMILIJA RAKIĆ PR EMILYS WORLD OF DESIGN
Address all correspondence to:

> Penmore Press LLC
> 920 N Javelina Pl
> Tucson AZ 85748

DEDICATION

For Anne

Our life together has been full of amazing memories. Here are a few from those hours when we were apart.

Pipeline Pig

Any device which is inserted into a pipeline and which travels freely through it, driven usually by the product flow. A "pig" is in effect a free moving piston.

Jim Cordell & Hershel Vanzant

Author's Note

Most industrial premises use a lot of pipework to convey products and services to where they are needed. In the oil, gas and chemicals industries in particular, pipework forms the hub of their operations. In order to maintain long distance pipelines, it is necessary to ensure that they remain clean and serviceable. One of the ways of doing this is to use "pipeline pigs". A pipeline pig is basically a piston which is temporarily inserted into the pipeline and propelled through it either by an inert gas (like nitrogen) or by the liquid or gas product in the pipeline. Pigging can be used to clean the pipelines either of solid deposits or to minimise cross contamination when the same pipeline is used for multiple products, such as different colours of paints or different product specifications.

Sophisticated "intelligent" pipeline pigs can be used to inspect the inside of a pipeline to ensure that it is not corroded, physically damaged or obstructed in some way. These pigs contain cameras, physical detectors or ultrasonic devices to remotely examine the condition of a pipeline and ensure that it remains capable of containing the liquids and gases being transported.

Now please read on....

Chapter 1

Clare felt the excitement. It was the first time for Steve and her, and she was nervous and sweating profusely. It was just her, Steve, and Bertha. What a threesome! She knelt by Bertha's hard metal bed and was aware she was screaming at the top of her voice. The vibrations! Suddenly Clare felt the earth move. Everything was shaking. She saw Steve rising up, his arms above his head. He was calling out but she couldn't hear.

Suddenly it was over. Steve clawed the big steam trip and throttle valve fully open. Three thousand, four hundred and fifty revs and they were through the criticals, when the big process gas compressor would bounce around, in danger of shaking itself to bits. She and Steve knew that to avoid damaging this massive machine they must start it up quickly and get the speed above the machine's natural frequency. It was there now. Ten tonnes of metal rotor purring like a tomcat. The noise was less of a rattle now, but trying to communicate with Steve was still like trying to order a beer inside a jet engine. Everything was sign language when your ears were encased in high performance ear defenders. Clare felt so good. It was the first time that she and Steve had been given the responsibility of starting up Big Bertha without the foreman supervising. She climbed down off the big machine's metal bed plate and gave a thumbs up to Steve. He beamed back.

Job done. Clare felt the relief and picked up her clipboard and set off to complete her routine process checks of oil pressures and bearing vibration readings. Big Bertha was old, but when she had been built, over 30 years before, she had been the world's largest double-ended centrifugal gas compressor. Three compressors driven out of both ends of a huge General Electric steam turbine. Everything on this chemical plant depended on the process gas compressor. When Bertha wasn't spinning, the plant didn't produce ethylene and the owners didn't make any money. If the owners didn't make money, Steve and Clare didn't have a job.

There had just been a problem elsewhere on the plant—in the hot end. The maintenance team had done wonders to sort out the problem on the boiler feed pump gearbox, but all the time that the plant was shut down, the furnaces were still producing process gas and it had to go somewhere. The safety precautions dictated that it went up the "chuff." The chuff was a 40-metre-high vertical flarestack and at full rates cost about £50 per minute of wasted gas, which was being burnt off and soared up into the wide blue yonder. Now that Clare had restarted Big Bertha, that £50 per minute was heading back into the coffers of the ever-hungry shareholders.

Clare had completed her rounds of the high-pressure compressor and was peering at the bearing oil sight glass on the turbine housing. Plenty of oil there. She moved her gloved hand onto the big steam pipe above the turbine casing. It felt abnormally hot. During the shutdown, an inspection engineer had removed some of the solid insulation to check on the condition of one of the high-pressure steam expansion bellows. She ran her skilled gloved hands caressingly up the outside of the bellows insulation. It should be cylindrical, but, wait, this one wasn't. It was barrel-shaped. Her mind flashed images of the bellows being about to give birth! Oh, my God! She yelled for Steve. He couldn't hear. She turned and ran for the big red mushroom-shaped emergency stop button. But too late. The

Duroc

bellows unit burst open in a gigantic fish mouth. Scalding and deafening high-pressure steam engulfed the entire compressor house in a searing white lethal cloud.

*****

It was quiet in the control room. Fraser sat in front of a long array of blinking computer screens. It could be quite tedious when the plant was running well. Before the plant had been taken over by Duroc, it would run for six years non-stop without the need for a major shutdown, but recently there seemed to be a lot of problems. He glanced to his left. Jack Milne was slouched in his chair doing a crossword. "Remote, fiery object in the sky?" he said.

"Sounds like a cryptic," replied Fraser.

"Aye."

"Maybe the first word's an anagram of remote—object in the sky—could be 'meteor.'"

"You always spoil it."

No sooner had Jack spoken than the computer screen lit up with red, as if a bleeding computer virus was invading the screen with alarms. The klaxon howled and the two panel operators sat bolt upright, their attention fixed on the screens.

"Low pressure in the de-propaniser."

"Must be a compressor trip."

"Aye," growled Jack. "First up trip is showing the compressor turbine's going down with loss of HP steam."

The control room door burst open. An outside operator yelled, "Man down! Get an ambulance! The turbine bellows have exploded! Clare and Steve are both in there!"

Fraser grabbed the phone and called in the emergency to the main gate. Jack didn't need any second bidding. He flipped the plant tannoy switch and called out, "Emergency team to the compressor deck—possible injured personnel!"

Simon W. Pain

*****

Martyn sat in his office gazing at the array of relics on his window sill. Each one was a trophy from a previous incident. Broken bearings, split gaskets, various valve spares, and a broken gearwheel. His job description as the plant's health and safety adviser gave him a wide range of responsibilities, but one of the most interesting was investigating accidents and damage. He turned to pick up the file on last month's injury and occupational health reports. He thumbed through the file nonchalantly and reflected on his job. If only the plant manager would listen to him and give him a bit more support. All he would ever say after an incident was, "How soon can we get back on line?" Never any enquiry about whether anyone had been hurt! It irritated Martyn. Sometimes the management's lack of empathy made him embarrassed. He felt embarrassed now. His cheek was flushed. Now his neck was red and he felt radiant heat spreading up the back of his head. He turned to the window. The sky was aflame with a smoky, red heat belching from the flarestack. He saw the steam jets on the flare tip come on with a thundering boom and the flame became intense as the smoke controls effectively quenched the smoke. Suddenly the phone jangled into life. "Southwick," he announced.

"Martyn, get yourself to the compressor deck," snapped Fraser. "There's been an explosion and Clare and Steve have been injured!"

Martyn grabbed his hardhat and ran off down the gloomy corridor towards the plant. Outside, the usual infernal din was diminishing, as the automatic safety controls were gradually shutting down the cold end of the process. He raced up the compressor house steps, taking them two at a time, up to the compressor deck. A first aider had already arrived. Clare was

Duroc

lying in a crumpled heap on the grating floor where she'd landed after the steam cloud had blown her off her feet. A first aider was bending over her, getting out a defibrillator. "Is the ambulance on its way?" Martyn demanded. The first aider didn't know. Martyn checked with the control room over his radio. The ambulance was five minutes away and he passed on the message to the first aider. "Anyone else hurt?" he yelled above the din.

"Yeah, Steve's over there, behind the overspeed governor panel."

Martyn found Steve, sitting dazed on the floor. "Where does it hurt?" he asked.

"I hit my back on the handrail, but I'm OK."

Now the cavalry was arriving. Another first aider started to check Steve over and Martyn stood up to take in the scene of devastation around the big turbine. There was debris everywhere. He wondered how this could have happened. Brodric Reynolds, the plant manager, appeared at the top of the access steps.

"Southwick," he yelled, "how could this happen? We've already lost two days' production with the boiler feed pump's failure!"

Martyn cringed. It was not his fault that the plant was shutting down yet again! He changed the subject. "Two injuries so far, sir. Clare looks pretty bad, but Steve may only have minor injuries. The ambulance is on its way."

As if by magic the sound of an ambulance siren wailed in the distance to confirm Martyn's allegation. He went back around the turbine to see how Clare was. She was still lying on the floor. "Keep clear!" cried the first aider as Clare's body shuddered with the electric shock from the defibrillator. No response. The first aider started CPR with rapid chest compressions. Every 30 compressions he stopped to deliver a "rescue breath". Then another shock from the defib. This time a response! Clare stirred. Her face was raw and bleeding from the sauna effect of the super-heated high-pressure steam. Her overalls were ripped and speckled with lagging dust and miscellaneous particles, which had presumably originally been part of the bellows. She didn't look good. Martyn looked away and saw Jack Milne leading two green-clad paramedics up the steps onto the compressor deck. The paramedics skilfully assessed Clare's injuries and then called for a stretcher—she needed a hospital, and quickly. It had only been 10 minutes since the bellows had failed and both Clare and Steve were being carried down to the ambulance, which was parked at a crazy angle in front of the gatehouse. Martyn noted the time. He might need that later. He turned to Brodric Reynolds and asked if he would be going to the hospital and if he would notify the next of kin.

"My job is running this plant, not acting as a nurse maid!" Brodric snapped and then stormed off to the control room. Martyn was torn—he needed to find out what had happened, but no one had gone to hospital with the injured operators. His training told him that it was "people first," and so he jogged back to the office to pick up his car keys and then made his way to the car park.

When Martyn walked into the hospital accident and emergency department, he went straight to the reception window. A rather overly made-up receptionist demanded to know his business. He explained that he was looking for the two recent emergency admissions from the Duroc Plant.

"Their names?"

"Clare Maxwell and Steve Bass."

The receptionist went away to check. She returned to tell him that both were in triage at the moment and couldn't be seen. Malcolm went to the waiting area and took out his mobile phone. He should ring the next of kin. He scrolled through his phone address book, and found Steve's home number.

"You can't use your phone in here!" called the receptionist in a rather haughty voice.

He would need to go outside. There was no answer to Steve's number, so he tried Clare's landline. The phone rang for a very long time, as it obviously switched to a mobile number.

"Hello. Callum Maxwell."

"Oh, hello, this is Martyn Southwick from Duroc. Are you Clare's husband?"

"No, I'm her father. Why do want to know?"

"I'm afraid that there's been an accident at the plant, and Clare is in hospital…"

There was a long pause and then Martyn explained what he knew about what had happened. After he had recovered a bit from the shock, Callum said that he would come straight away and be in the hospital within 20 minutes. Martyn returned to the waiting room and got a black coffee from the vending machine. He thought about what might have gone wrong at the plant. It was just another in a string of incidents since Duroc had taken over the plant. He tried to think about how he would investigate this latest incident so that he could ensure that it wouldn't happen again. He looked around the room. The digital clock said "18:45." He realised that he should have been home by now. He would call his wife and probably get another ear bending, as she never understood the importance of his job!

"Mr Southwick." the receptionist's haughty voice boomed around the waiting room. He looked up. The phone call to his wife would have to wait.

"Yes?"

"Miss Maxwell is being admitted to one of the wards, but Mr Bass can go home," was the imperious reply.

After a short wait Steve Bass ambled awkwardly into the waiting room. Martyn waved. "What's the damage?"

"Oh! I'm OK. The back is a bit sore, but I'll live." Steve grinned. "How's Clare?"

Martyn told him that she had been admitted to the wards but he didn't yet know anything more, and so he offered to take Steve home. He thought that they might be able to talk on the way.

The 25-minute car journey didn't reveal anything very interesting. Steve and Clare had been starting up Big Bertha following the two-day maintenance shutdown. Although it was the first time that they had done it unsupervised, they had both assisted with machine start-ups before and there had been nothing unusual on this occasion. The start-up of the turbo compressor had gone without incident, and Steve said that he and Clare had just begun their routine checks. Clare had been doing the turbine checks and he'd been looking over the three compressors. He thought that Clare had been near the HP Steam inlet to the turbine when it had exploded. But he couldn't be sure of her exact position because he'd been attending to the high-pressure compressor at the time. The blast of steam had knocked him against the compressor deck hand rail, which was why his back had been injured. Steve surmised that the escaping steam from the turbine meant that the revs would drop and the automatic detection systems would sound the alarms and then trip the machine. He confirmed that he had not manually stopped Big Bertha.

The car pulled up outside Steve's house. "Do you want me to come in with you?" Martyn asked.

"No, I'll be alright. Is Clare going to be OK, do you think?"

Martyn thought that he detected some moisture around Steve's eyes. "I'll check in the morning and let you know," he

Duroc

replied, and then continued, "Could you write down what you remember and let me have a copy, please?"

Steve agreed and with a bit of a groan pulled himself out of the car and limped to the front door.

Chapter 2

Apprentice Dougie Watson had three interests in life: girls, football, and a Kawasaki KX450-SR off road bike. The interest was very much in reverse order. This meant that he had very little interest in completing the fourth year of his apprenticeship. Work was boring! Today he was being mentored by Jim Cleary, a rather ponderous, but very cautious, middle-aged fitter, and they were working in the storage area, apparently doing something called "pigging." He had no idea what that was, but management had told him that that was why he was there—to learn.

They had been to the control room to collect a permit to allow them to carry out the pigging job safely. Jim explained that they were needing to purge a pipeline of heavy oil, because some sections of it were worn and needed to be replaced. He explained that if there was any oil left in the pipeline when they started to cut out the worn sections and weld in new ones, then it had a slight tendency to go bang! Apparently, this was not a good idea. In order to clean and prepare the pipeline for cutting and welding, the pipe had been drained of oil by the process operators. But the pipe was nearly a mile long and went up hill and down dale, so not all the oil could be drained out. The job today was to put a "pig" into the line. Jim explained that there were lots of different designs of "pigs." He said that today they would be using a foam pig.

Duroc

"Does it squeal?" asked Dougie, sniggering under his breath.

Jim ignored him and went on to explain that early pigs had been made from straw, barbed wire and leather, and that the term "pig" was actually an acronym for "Pipeline Inspection Gauge." Dougie yawned.

Jim was irritated. Here he was trying to impart some of his wisdom and the youngster wasn't even interested. He would make sure that Dougie did most of the physical work! They began by cycling up to the discharge end of the pipe where they connected a flexible hose to a suitable drain point and diverted the hose to a collection tank. They then cycled the mile back to the storage area and carefully disconnected a flange to provide an access point for the foam pig. Dougie was then instructed to seal the open end of the pipe behind the pig with a blank flange. The flange had a small connection on it to allow gas to be introduced behind the pig. This gas is what would push the pig along the inside of the pipe like a piston. Jim claimed that any residual oil that was in the pipeline would be pushed out ahead of the pig. The danger was that if compressed air was used to propel the pig, the combination of air and oil could create an explosive atmosphere and the pipe could unzip and take them with it! Jim explained that they would use an inert gas to ensure that there was no risk of explosion. He told Dougie to connect the gas inlet hose to the nearby nitrogen supply. Dougie dragged the hose over the pipe trench and called out, "Is this the nitrogen supply?"

"No—it's the black pipe by that big redundant tank."

*****

Martyn arrived at work at 8 o'clock. As he switched his radio on, he received a call from Jim Cleary about a pigging job that was going on in the storage area. He discussed the job with

Jim for a few minutes before confirming that he was happy for it to go ahead, especially as the plant was now shut down following yesterday's compressor incident. Martyn donned his hard hat and hi-vis jacket and set off towards the compressor house to start his investigation. Then he remembered that he had not reported the incident to Ashe, and so he turned back and made the phone call. "Ashe" was an acronym for the Alba Safety & Health Executive—the Scottish safety regulator. He left a message on the answer phone for Bluey Scrimshaw, the Ashe inspector responsible for the east coast of Scotland.

Martyn arrived in the quiet compressor house at 8:15am. The area was already taped off and the compression engineer was there, carefully examining the damaged turbine.

"Morning, Martyn."

"Hi, Iain—any news about Clare?"

"Nothing yet."

"What do you reckon happened?"

"Well, the bellows burst. It wasn't an explosion, and there was no pressure increase shown on the data logger. It looks as though the bellows just failed under normal steam pressure."

"Must have been a faulty bellows?" queried Martyn.

"Could be—we would need the metallurgists to look at the pieces to see if there was any sign of fatigue or manufacturing faults."

"Before you take stuff away, I'd like to get some photographs," Martyn said.

He left for the control room to get a permit to use his battery-powered camera and returned to take the photographs. The great thing about modern digital cameras was that you didn't need to be a Lord Litchfield, you just took loads of snaps and deleted those which were either no good or not needed.

Iain, the compression engineer, was still ferreting around in the debris as Martyn was about to leave. "Brodric's called a meeting at 10 o'clock in the upstairs conference room to talk about plant restart," he said. "Are you going?"

"Not been invited—which is not that unusual—but I'll be there," replied Martyn as he made towards the stairs leading down from the compressor deck.

The conference room was full. Martyn found it difficult to find a chair. Brodric Reynolds sat glowering at the head of the table, surrounded by used coffee cups. He was not happy. He reminded the assembled throng that time was money, and that there was a need to get the plant re-commissioned as soon as possible. He immediately started talking about the programme for start-up, purging this and re-inventorying that. Martyn wondered if anyone knew what Brodric was talking about. Martyn was a naturally nervous and cautious character, but Reynolds was jumping the gun. No one had asked about Clare or Steve—it seemed that they were just collateral damage of no real concern.

"Could I suggest that before we talk about re-starting the plant, we need to understand what happened yesterday and make sure that we can eliminate the root cause?" Martyn offered.

Luckily, Iain had just arrived. He reminded Reynolds that there were two bellows on the turbine, and said that he agreed with Martyn, that they needed to understand what had gone wrong, otherwise the second bellows might suffer the same fate. There was a need to properly investigate the incident before it would be safe to restart Big Bertha.

Reynolds was furious. His face turned a strange, blotchy purple colour. Martyn thought he might explode, like the bellows! Instead, as he sprang up, his chair fell backwards with a crash. "You can have until this afternoon, and then the plant restarts," he announced. He turned and stormed out of the room, tripping over the raised chair leg. This rather spoilt the effect, as he exited head-first, in a near horizontal mode, much to everyone's silent delight! Somebody muttered, "Mind the chair!" under their breath.

Martyn looked at Iain, who was smothering a grin. "I need to go and find out how Clare is, and see if she can tell us anything," Martyn said. "Can you see if you can find out if there was anything untoward about the bellows?"

"Yes, leave it with me, and give my regards to Clare," said Iain.

The drive to the hospital was uneventful, but progress was delayed by a stop-off at a small roadside green grocer's stall to purchase some grapes.

There was something odd about yesterday's incident, and Martyn couldn't quite put his finger on it. As he drew into the car park, his mobile phone rang. He pulled into a parking space and picked up the phone. The screen said that the caller was "Ashe."

*****

The Alba Safety & Health Executive office was a three-storey, 1960s-style building on the outskirts of Falkirk. The building was past its best. It had the typical flat roof with lots of glass and flaking paintwork. Half the ground floor of the building was a covered car park. Arbuthnot Scrimshaw drove into his usual parking space. He was a fit, middle-aged Lancashire man with 10 years at "the Executive." He enjoyed life, but didn't appreciate the Christian name that his parents had lumbered him with. He'd had his leg pulled mercilessly at school about the name, until one day during an art lesson the art master had explained to the class that the unusual art of carving whale bones was called "scrimshaw." Thereafter Arbuthnot was called "the

Duroc

Blue Whale"! This eventually was shortened by his kinder friends to "Bluey," and that nickname had stuck.

Bluey walked into the large open-plan office on the first floor, dropped his briefcase by his desk and went to the kitchenette to get a cup of coffee. "Morning, Millie," he said to one of the other health and safety inspectors as he poured himself a large mug of black coffee. *That should wake me up*, he thought. He drifted back to his desk, logged on to his desk computer and started to scroll through the usual interminable list of emails. He scanned the list and picked out one from the Incident Contact Centre. He opened the email and read that Duroc Petrochemicals Ltd had reported a steam pressure release that had resulted in two hospitalisations. That needed some investigation. Bluey spun his rolodex and drew out the card with the phone number of Duroc. The contact was the health and safety adviser, a Martyn Southwick. He dialled the number.

Martyn's mobile phone rang. "Duroc Petrochemicals, Southwick speaking." It was Ashe. The inspector was called Scrimshaw but Martyn knew him as "Bluey." He had met him once before. Martyn briefly summarised what he knew of the incident, and explained that the plant was shut down as a result of the incident. One of the victims of the incident had been discharged from hospital, but the other, a Miss Clare Maxwell, had been admitted to the hospital overnight. Martyn added that he was just on his way to go and visit her to get a statement. Bluey said that he would like to be present when the statement was taken. It would take him about 20 minutes to drive to the hospital and they could meet up in reception and go to see her together.

Martyn drove around to the hospital's main entrance. The receptionist was much more pleasant than the one in A&E had been the day before. She directed Martyn to Ward 3, where he should find Miss Maxwell. She said that visiting was allowed any time. As they were talking, Bluey Scrimshaw from Ashe arrived, and after the initial pleasantries they took the large lift together up to Ward 3. At the ward, they had to check in at the nurses' station and so Martyn took the opportunity to ask how Clare was.

"Are you a relative?"

"No, I represent her employer."

The pleasant young nurse took a file from under the desk and flipped the pages. "I have only just come on shift," she apologised. Then, reading from the file, she told them that Clare was out of danger and improving. They were warned that Clare had quite extensive burns to her face and arms and so she was heavily bandaged. They would find Clare in the bed beside the window in the room at the end of the ward, but were warned not to tire her.

Clare looked every bit like an Egyptian mummy. The head bandaging had spaces for eyes and mouth, but not much else. Slightly embarrassed, Martyn proffered the grapes and asked how she was. She had been better, she said, but at least she could talk and eat grapes!

Bluey explained who he was and asked her about what had happened.

"Where do you want me to start?" she asked.

"Well, go back as far as you think is relevant," Bluey replied.

"I'll tell you about the incident first, but I think things go back before yesterday."

Martyn was intrigued. Clare told them more or less the same story about the bellows failure that he had heard yesterday from Steve Bass. There really wasn't much to tell, as it had all happened so fast.

Duroc

"Why do you think that the cause might be before yesterday?" he asked.

"I don't know. It just seems odd that they were working on that very same bellows just before we restarted Big Bertha," she said.

"What was happening on the bellows?" asked Bluey.

"I'm not too sure," Clare replied. "It was during the emergency shutdown to deal with the boiler feed water pump gearbox repair. It just suddenly cropped up. We were just about to restart when the fitters came along with a permit to dismantle and inspect the bellows. The odd thing was that the permit was for inspection of both bellows, but they only did one. After they had removed the bellows unit on the left-hand side of the turbine, they said that they'd taken a message telling them to put it back, and not to worry about the bellows on the right-hand side."

"Are these bellows inspected very often?" asked Bluey.

"I've never seen or heard of it being done in my time—that is, in the last five years," answered Clare. "What was also odd is that they almost threw the bellows back together. It was real 'gung-ho' stuff!"

"Was it the bellows that blew up?" Bluey asked.

Clare said again that she wasn't sure, but she'd been near the turbine when something blew her off her feet. She had assumed that because they'd just been working on the bellows, that that was probably the cause of the explosion. "No—wait! It *must* have been the bellows, because I felt it with my hand and its shape was distorted!"

"Do you know who the technicians were and what they actually did?" said Martyn.

"It was just one technician working on the bellows—that new bloke who used to work offshore."

"Carl Dunne? He started with us just a few weeks ago."

Bluey seemed to wake up. "We need talk to Mr Dunn—is he at work today?"

The two men took their leave of Clare and quickly headed back to the hospital car park, then they drove in tandem back to the Duroc plant. Martyn had phoned ahead and found that Carl Dunne was at work today and would be available to speak with them as soon as they arrived. Bluey wanted to see the turbine bellows unit before speaking with Dunne and so they headed directly to the compressor house. The turbine was still shut down and surrounded by billowing black and yellow tape. They found Iain Talbot, the compression engineer, examining the undamaged bellows unit. He explained to Bluey that the bends of the bellows were called "convolutions" and that when in use the inner convolutions should be supported by a clamp to prevent them blowing outwards under the steam pressure. Iain showed Bluey that each concave convolution had a clamp in the form of a support ring. However, he had noticed that in amongst the debris following the failure, so far, he could only find the remains of five support rings, whereas the bellows had six convolutions. If there were six convolutions, there should be six support rings! Iain was suspicious. He thought that the missing support ring could have been left out on purpose. If that was the case, then this failure might have been sabotage, because no competent technician would leave out a support ring by accident.

"Why did no one else notice?" asked Bluey.

"Once the insulation is replaced, no one can tell whether the support rings are there or not," said Iain.

The three men carefully sifted through the debris around the turbine casing. Iain was right—there was no evidence of the sixth support ring. Iain showed the others the remains of the other support rings. They were doughnut-shaped rings, split in half and held together by just two long bolts. Bluey thought that

Duroc

it would be quick and easy to remove a single ring and put the parts into your tool bag.

Bluey turned to Iain and said, "Can you get the undamaged bellows inspected? In particular, get it crack-detected to see if that was about to fail as well." Then he declared to Martyn, "Time to meet Mr Dunne."

Carl Dunne had worked for years as an oil rig worker—what the Americans would call a "roustabout." However, Carl was no Yankee. He was a tough, albeit reticent Aberdonian, whose wife had got tired of North Sea rig contracts and insisted that he get a less transient lifestyle on the mainland. Hence his move to Duroc just three weeks before.

Martyn introduced Bluey as the health and safety inspector from Ashe. Carl grunted. Bluey asked about the bellows inspection and how the job had arisen. Carl explained in as few words as possible that he had been told to check the bellows.

"Who by?" asked Bluey.

"The gaffer."

"Who's that?"

"Reynolds—calls his sel' Brodric! He's the high-heid yin."

Martyn explained to Bluey that Brodric Reynolds was the plant manager.

"What were you asked to do?"

"Jiust tae inspect th' billuws."

"Yes, but what did you actually do?"

"'Twas gey short notice. He juist said, 'Gang 'n' keek at th' billuws—'n' tak' yer time.'"

"And then what?"

"A' soon as th' lagging 'n' rings wur aff, th' control room radioed me taew pat it back th'gither."

"Did you refit all the support rings?"

"Aye."

"Carl, where did you work before coming here to Duroc?" asked Bluey.

"I've aye worked for Duroc. Afore th' guidwife nagged me tae gut a jab oan shore."

So Carl Dunne previously worked for Duroc Offshore, thought Bluey.

Further questioning was not very fruitful, or even very coherent, and so after a brief but futile summary, Martyn and Bluey left and went to the workshop in search of the maintenance supervisor.

The supervisor was a wiry character who went by the easily distinguishable name of "Mac"—along with half the workforce! In the event of confusion, which generally happened about 20 times per hour, this Mac was "Big Mac," which belied his size but reflected his taste for fast food. Big Mac explained that there had been an emergency shutdown of the plant because the last boiler feed pump had finally given up the ghost. He didn't know anything about a job on the turbine bellows. It had not been on the shutdown work-list. However, he said that there had been something odd about the boiler feed water pump.

Bluey focused on the bellows. "Was there some problem with the bellows that would cause Carl to have to check it?"

"Not that I was aware of. Bellows problems are very rare indeed. Usually, the only thing that can go wrong is fatigue, which might lead to a crack and a small steam leak, but it wouldn't be catastrophic, so that repairs could be done in a planned way. In any case, if there was a suspicion about the condition of the bellows, it would be common sense to check them both and not just one."

Bluey wondered about the missing support ring. "If the technician removed the six support rings but only replaced five, where would the missing ring have been left?"

Duroc

"Well, during the inspection, the rings and bolts would probably have been put on the floor. So either the missing ring will be on the compressor house floor, or in the scrap skip."

"Well, it's not on the floor," said Bluey.

Big Mac suggested that they go and check the skip. The scrap metal skip was just outside the main roller-shutter door of the workshop. The skip was full of a huge array of old and damaged machine components. Big Mac picked up a length of scrap rod and started to rummage around amongst the components, looking for the ring.

Martyn pointed further back in the skip. There, partially hidden by several rusty pipe flanges, was half of a bellows support ring. "I think Mr Dunne has some more questions to answer!" he said.

Chapter 3

It was Saturday and Debbie Scrimshaw sat down for breakfast. There was no school today for the children. She enjoyed weekends, as things were less hectic and the boys didn't need to be coaxed off to school. They had finished their breakfast and were already getting dressed. Bluey was taking the boys to football club in a few minutes' time. She would be able to relax and quietly read the *Daily Record* for a few minutes and catch up on the latest news. She picked up the paper and spread it on the table beside her. Reaching across for some marmalade, she buttered the toast and munched her way through it.

The headlines were about a motorway crash in the central belt that had tragically killed a pensioner and a lorry driver. The news was always so depressing! She searched for some positive news. The Scottish Government were planning to invest in more windfarms and a revolutionary tidal turbine system just offshore from Sullom Voe. It fulfilled the positive news criteria—but interesting? No. She turned the page, scattering toast crumbs onto the tablecloth. She read the headline.

SCOTTISH DRUGS DEATH SHOCK

She knew that Scotland had a drug problem and she worried that it would only be eight years before her two babies would be going off to university and have to fend for themselves in the big, bad world. She read on. The article claimed that Scotland

Duroc

had proportionally more deaths from drugs than the rest of the UK, and in fact more than anywhere else in Europe. It appeared that one of the problems was that the supply of drugs had increased dramatically in the last few months, and this was being distributed via the "county lines"—not just to the major conurbations of Glasgow and Edinburgh, but also around the small towns and villages. The drugs were being imported into the country and supply was rife. The police had clamped down on trafficking across the border with England and the Coastguard and Customs people were watching the coast. However, despite their best efforts the supply appeared to have shot up and law enforcement was going backwards.

At that moment the boys bounced into the room, followed by their dad. Debbie looked up at Bluey. "Have you seen this article?" she asked. "I hadn't realised what a huge increase had occurred in drugs trafficking recently."

Bluey quickly scanned the article. He knew most of the stuff already, but he was surprised at the recent upsurge in trafficking. "Yeah, it's quite a problem,' he replied, "but not really part of Ashe's domain. I'll see you later. After I've dropped the boys off at footie, I'll drop into the office for an hour." And so, with a quick peck on Debbie's cheek, he was off with the over-hyped boys.

Bluey dropped the boys off at the junior football club at Stenhousemuir, and then he made his way to the office in Falkirk to catch up on some paperwork. The bleak office was even worse on a Saturday when no one else was there. It reminded him of a condemned school! He completed the weekly reports on the events of the last few days and sat for a moment to relish a polystyrene cup of so-called coffee and to twiddle with his Rubik's cube. Suddenly the doors to the open-plan office burst open and his boss barged in wearing a rather too-tight tracksuit showing unsightly sweat stains.

"Hi, Bluey," he gasped. "Didn't know you'd be here."

"Just catching up on last week's admin," said Bluey.

"What's going on at Duroc?"

"On the face of it, looks like an un-planned steam escape from a failed bellows unit. One female hospitalised. But there's more to it, I'm sure. I'm not getting the truth from the tradesman involved and there's something odd about the circumstances. Too many things happening at the same time for my liking." He clicked the Rubik's cube.

"Do you need more help?" asked his boss.

"Maybe. I'll see how things go."

"Well, young Caitlin can help you if you need an extra pair of hands."

Caitlin Barland was a young graduate trainee who had been with Ashe for about six months. She was very bright and had a first-class degree from St Andrews University in Interdisciplinary Studies, whatever that was. Bluey liked her and found that she had a very incisive brain. She was keen to learn. She was also very easy on the eye.

"It would be a good learning experience for her" he replied spinning up a full side of orange squares on his Rubik's cube, pretending not to be too enthusiastic. He had found that the clue to solving the Rubick's Cube was to remember that the centre square on any side of the cube never moves, and so that defines the colour needed on that side! After that it was just logistics!

His boss nodded and went on to collapse in his office and recover from his run. Bluey thought that his boss was obviously not in any hurry to get home—was there a domestic problem?

The computer pinged to announce the arrival of email. It was from Iain at Duroc Petrochemicals. Iain had completed the crack detection of the remains of the bellows, and he had also checked the second undamaged bellows. *Good man*, thought

Duroc

Bluey. Apparently, there was no sign of cracks in the bellows metal and so Iain had surmised that there was no suggestion of fatigue. So why had it been necessary to inspect the bellows?

So far Carl Dunne was the only one who knew anything about the bellows inspection and it was clear that he was not telling the truth. Bluey made a mental note to re-interview him. He also wanted to know more about the reason for the plant emergency shutdown following the boiler feedwater pump failure. He sent a message to Iain and copied it to Martyn Southwick, asking for details of the boiler feedwater pump problem. He told Martyn that he would be at Duroc again tomorrow and would like to meet with Carl Dunne and also the plant manager.

*****

Leaves fluttered gently to the ground as the morning sky burst into a glowing furnace of crimson. It was peaceful at that time of the morning and a small herd of Belted Galloway cattle, displaying their trademark broad white band, stirred nonchalantly on the lush green pasture. A road-side speed limit roundel was losing the battle against the ever-encroaching hedgerow. All was quiet and there was barely a sound from the empty road, that snaked down from Jawcraig into Lochgreen. Over the hill there was a burst of noise. It was too loud for a car, and revving too fast for a tractor or truck. Suddenly a vivid green machine on two wheels roared into sight. As the machine hit the snaking bends it angled first left and then right. It roared past Westerglen Farm; one of the "Belties" looked up but failed to comprehend the angled word "Triumph" and "Tiger 950 Sport". If the cattle couldn't recognise the motorbike, then the bike rider certainly didn't react to the speed limit sign— probably because the "40" was just a blur, as the machine flew by at twice that speed! There was a sharp right-hand bend as the town of Falkirk appeared in the distance. The bike was going too fast into the 90 degree bend! At the last minute the rider braked with a screech and shed 20 mph, but it wasn't enough. The rear wheel lost grip on the road and fired loose gravel into the hedgerow. The young rider swerved to compensate, bounced off the opposite verge and twisted on more power.

Moments later the big Triumph approached the built-up area. A speed activated dot matrix sign on the road verge flashed the words "SLOW DOWN". It had no effect. But then school children. Older ones talking in groups on the pavement, oblivious to the traffic. Finally, the machine slowed to a speed that was approximately legal. The bike came to a halt at the cross roads. The traffic lights were on red. Toddlers bounced across the road tethered to their Mum's hands. They looked at the rider. All they saw was a dark visor, some flowing golden locks and a large black ace of spades motif on the lurid green helmet. But they all knew who it was, and they all waved madly. She smiled to herself and waved back. The lights flipped to green and she sped off to another day's work.

The girl parked her bike in the car park and strode into the offices, removing her helmet as she went. She swiped her security access card by the door and ran up the stairs to the open-plan office where she worked. She tossed her lurid green motorcycle helmet with the ace of spades motif onto her desk.

"Morning Caitlin" smiled Bluey, "Grab your stuff, we're on a shout. An incident at Duroc Petrochemicals"

On the drive to the Duroc plant he explained to her what had happened. It seemed quite straight forward, but he felt that something was not right and that was why he wanted another pair of eyes involved. Caitlin's job was to use her interdisciplinary studies background in psychology and mechanical engineering to observe how people reacted. They parked in the main car park inside the factory gate and were met by Martyn Southwick. Bluey introduced Caitlin and then they went into the administration building to wait for Brodric Reynolds, the plant manager, who was temporarily delayed at the morning meeting.

They sat in the upstairs conference room, which was still littered with old coffee cups. Whilst they waited, Bluey asked about the recent shutdown.

Martyn said that the shutdown had been unplanned and had happened at short notice. He explained that they had two large boiler feedwater pumps in the hot end of the plant which fed water through to the steam boilers. The plant could not operate without a steam supply, and so it was critically important that at least one of those was running. One of the two pumps had been out of action for several weeks and was undergoing major repairs. Bluey asked what the problem was. Martyn said he didn't know, but he would find out.

However, the problem last Tuesday night had been that the only remaining pump had suddenly developed a very noisy gearbox. The maintenance team had recommended that it be shut down before it did more serious damage. This meant a full and expensive shutdown of the whole plant. Martyn was unsure of the detail of what repairs were necessary, and so he rang Iain and put him on the phone's loudspeaker.

"Morning, Iain. I have got two inspectors here from Ashe and we're discussing the boiler feed water pump breakdown. They would like to know what you found."

"Well, there was only one pump available," Iain said, "because the standby was undergoing a major rebuild. That entailed removing and rebuilding the pump multi-stage impeller shaft. It was a big job and we were short of both labour and spares, so it was likely to be at least another week before that one was ready. But I wasn't unduly concerned, because the good pump had only just been fully overhauled."

"So, the problems with the gearbox were a surprise?" said Bluey.

"They certainly were. Usually, unless it's a catastrophic failure, like something breaks, we get warning of deterioration, as the vibration and noise tend to increase."

"What do you think happened?"

"When the fitters opened up the gearbox, they found that the oil had emulsified. My first thought was that water from the pump body had escaped and spilled into the gearbox, but the operators were adamant that there had been no water leak. The pump is well protected from the weather, and so the only other way that water could get in there would be if someone put it there on purpose."

"You mean sabotage?" asked Bluey. He looked at Caitlin.

She said, "Why would anyone want to sabotage the plant? It doesn't make sense."

At that moment the door burst open and a very red-faced Brodric Reynolds exploded into the room. Bluey half rose and offered his hand by way of introduction.

"Why are you stopping me from re-starting the plant?" growled Reynolds.

Bluey ignored his question. "I'm Bluey Scrimshaw, the area inspector from Ashe," he said. "And this is my colleague, Caitlin Barland. The plant will not re-start until my colleague and I are satisfied that we understand what went wrong and that you have put actions in place to prevent it recurring."

Caitlin thought that Brodric Reynolds was going to hit Bluey.

"If it is necessary, I can issue you with an enforcement notice," Bluey added.

Reynolds mellowed a little and slowly subsided into a chair.

"Shall I get some coffee?" said Martyn as he beat a hasty retreat.

Duroc

They sat in stony silence until Martyn returned with four coffees. He carefully gave Brodric the mug bearing the logo "I could agree with you, but then we'd both be wrong." It didn't raise a smile. After an interminable pause, as if by magic, Brodric and Bluey both started speaking at once. Reynolds backed off.

"How are Clare Maxwell and Steve Bass?" asked Bluey.

Reynolds looked blankly at Martyn Southwick, as if diverting the question to him.

"Steve is back home with just a minor back strain, but it looks as though Miss Maxwell will be in hospital for a few days. However, her prognosis is good. We'll be declaring this as a lost-time injury, as she could be off for several weeks whilst the burns heal," reported Martyn.

"I suppose she'll be after compensation," said Reynolds under his breath.

But Caitlin heard. "I would have thought that your first thought would be for the wellbeing of your employees!" she snapped.

Bluey frowned at her. It wasn't their job to antagonise.

"So, when can we restart the plant?" said Reynolds again, glowering at Caitlin. "Every hour costs us money!"

"Not at the moment, Brodric!" Everyone had forgotten that Iain was still on the speakerphone and no one had dropped the call. His voice echoed around the conference room. "You might remember, Brodric, that the feedstock tank is empty, and that without feedstock we cannot re-start. The North Sea pipeline has only just started flowing again. We were just about running on fumes before we shut down to repair the boiler feedwater pump, so if that hadn't happened, we would have come off-line anyway."

Caitlin thought she saw Reynolds squirm. Bluey raised an eyebrow at her. So, what was going on? It seemed that the man in charge of production didn't know he had run out of feedstock—either that or for some reason he was keeping it very quiet.

"How is it that a plant of this size, which relies on continuous production, has apparently run out of feedstock?" asked Bluey.

"Times are hard," replied Reynolds.

"Does that mean you have a bit of a cash flow crisis?"

"Money has been difficult since Duroc took over the plant nine months ago."

"Can't you fund the feedstock, then?"

"Yes, we've just had a cash injection from a benefactor, but there's also been some problems with the under-sea pipeline, which meant that we've not been able to replenish stocks."

Bluey remembered that Iain had told him that one of the delays causing the boiler feedwater pump shutdown was lack of spares and labour. Was Duroc in financial trouble? He changed the subject now that Reynolds was being more reasonable. "You need to establish the cause of the bellows failure and undertake competent repairs before the plant restarts," he said.

Iain spoke up from the speaker-phone. "We've established that not all the support rings were replaced on the bellows. There was nothing wrong with the bellows itself, but without one of the support rings, the bellows would balloon outwards and failure would then be inevitable."

"Why was a support ring left off?" boomed Brodric.

"We won't know until we have spoken again with Carl Dunne." Came the answer from the speaker phone.

"Miss Barland and I would like to be there when you talk to Mr Dunne," said Bluey.

"That's fine," Iain replied. "It will be his break anytime now, and we can talk to him then. I'll meet you both in the foreman's office in 10 minutes' time." The speakerphone clicked and Iain was gone.

Bluey went on: "We understand from Iain that the previous shutdown caused by the boiler feedwater pump gearbox failure might have been sabotage?"

"That's news to me," responded Reynolds.

"Iain seems to think that water had been added to the gearbox oil, causing the gears to seize up."

"You'll need to talk to him about that," Reynolds said. A secretary entered the room with a waft of light floral perfume and handed Brodric a scribbled post-it note. With an impolite grunt he got up and left the room.

"I think this session has just ended," quipped Bluey, and Caitlin, Martyn and he left in search of the workshop foreman's office.

The four of them stood crowded into the small office. Carl Dunne was seated at the side of the desk. He had his union representative with him. Communication with the broad-speaking Scot was a bit of a challenge. It turned out that the bellows inspection had not been a planned or scheduled job. It seemed to have been a very last-minute decision.

Bluey questioned Carl about why he had done the job. Initially he suggested that it had been his own decision to carry it out, but when Caitlin enquired about what he had been doing immediately before the work on the bellows, he admitted that the previous job had been abandoned part way through so that he could go to the compressor house.

"So, who instructed you to change tasks?" Bluey asked.

Bluey thought that the discussion was becoming significant and so he told Carl that he was now being interviewed "under caution." The union representative was furious and thereafter all Dunne's responses consisted of a noncommittal "no comment." After that, any further discussion was pointless and the investigating trio left the hostile atmosphere of the office and went out into the workshop area.

Martyn took Bluey and Caitlin over to see the damaged internal gears that had been removed during the boiler feedwater pump overhaul. The gears were rusty and it was obvious that they had suffered from lack of lubrication. Bluey thought that it did look like sabotage. Was it connected in any way to the bellows failure, he wondered, or was it just indicative that standards were not very high at Duroc? Either way it was an issue.

Bluey and Caitlin had done as much as they could at the plant and so they took their leave of Martyn and headed back to the office in Falkirk.

*****

The sun shone in through the large picture window, scattering amber and yellow light across the room. Newspapers were strewn across the huge oak desk. Moura lounged in his reclining chair, looking as though he would topple over backwards at any moment. Of course, his name was not Moura—that was just a cover. His wife and family wouldn't use that name—in fact they wouldn't even recognise it. Nor would the tax man. But things were not going well. The usually trouble-free process of his most lucrative business was going through a rocky patch. It had been a gold mine, but now everything that could go wrong, was going wrong. Some of his rather questionable acquaintances were proving to be unreliable. They would have to be dealt with. Some of the "muppets" that they used to get stuff done were worse than useless. Too many mistakes were being made and that affected his income, and cascaded down to some of his other legitimate business interests. Last week's secure shipment had gone badly wrong in a way that neither he nor anyone else had predicted. The plan had appeared to be faultless, and undetectable, but now there was a major problem. He needed new assets and he had his eye on a major UK-wide acquisition that would transform his business and keep it under cover.

Moura picked up the burner phone and waited for the scrambled secure connection.

Chapter 4

The yellow, luffing jib of the big post crane was silhouetted against the bleak grey skies. Below bobbed the vivid orange hull of the oil rig support vessel in stark contrast to the boiling, charcoal-coloured sea. The ship was held on station by its azimuth thrusters, which were operating off a satellite positioner. Her crew were offloading the latest batch of supplies and spare parts onto the rig. Gannet Gamma was an integrated rig in the Gamma field of the North Sea sited about 100 miles east of Aberdeen. The 200 offshore workers who knew the rig as home for two weeks at a time fondly called it the "GG." The installation was made up of three separate platforms linked by what appeared to be rather flimsy walkways high above the sea, which connected the drilling platform to the production platform and the accommodation block.

The morning meeting had just broken up and there was a buzz of activity. Orange-clad figures with yellow helmets were now spreading like ants around the congested decks and walkways of the rig. Moray Stewart was production area supervisor and was responsible for all the activities on the production platform. The main purpose was to process the crude oil from the wells and separate it into lighter products for transfer to shore through the two big undersea pipelines. Moray was also responsible for housekeeping on the rig. Often this was the biggest challenge because space was so cramped. When new stores arrived, the previous crates and stillages had to be lifted off first to ensure that there was enough room to land the new stuff. Just at the moment, this was a particular problem as there were significant engineering projects going on and there wasn't really enough room for all the new pipes and equipment that needed to be offloaded, let alone for all the day-to-day stores and food.

Moray radioed the first mate on the support vessel. He had received the full manifest during the morning meeting and knew what needed to be offloaded both from the GG and the ship. It was a tricky operation, as the crane carefully picked up empty crates and cradles from the rig and came back with a full load. It was a really skilled job, because the crane driver was so high up that he couldn't see the deck of the supply ship or even some parts of the deck where crates needed to be stored. Everything was done by radio contact. Moray was overseeing the work on the rig and he left it to the first mate to ensure that the right loads got lifted from the ship's deck.

They worked throughout much of the morning, halting at one stage as a Sikorsky S-92 thundered onto the helipad. The crane unloaded crate after crate of food, engineering spares, contractor's pigs, light fittings, and various spaghetti forms of pre-fabricated pipework. Eventually all the empties were gone and there were great stacks of new supplies piled two or three high all over the deck. The clever thing was to know exactly where everything was and to ensure that the first thing to be needed was on top!

Moray dropped down the stairway from the upper deck and wound his way back to the control room in the lower deck house. The supplies unloading had gone well. He made his way through the narrow corridors to the cramped control room. He dropped into a vacant chair and scanned the computer displays that told him the state of the various stages of oil processing.

"There's a spec change coming up on the USP1," said the lead operator.

Moray knew that this meant that the specification of the oil that was being exported from the rig would be changing. The USP was the undersea pipeline.

"Does that mean launching the pigs?" he asked.

"Aye, the pigs have just arrived and been offloaded onto the main deck. When are the 'Drifters' due?"

"Just called through—they're leaving Aberdeen any time now. They'll be on the 4 o'clock chopper."

Moray knew the pigging contractors. They were regular visitors to the GG. On the rig they were known as the "Drifters." It was a take-off of the name of a group of pigs and was meant to be derogatory!

"There seem to have been an awful lot of pigging jobs recently," reflected the lead operator.

Moray just grunted. He picked up a three-day-old newspaper. The newspapers were always a day or two out of date. There wasn't much of interest. He turned to the back page and read about the latest trouble at the "Old Firm" game. Not too bad—just 20 arrests this time! Scanning forwards through the crumpled pages he saw plenty of adverts for holidays in Spain, but he always left those arrangements to his wife. He would just turn up on the day. He read an article about some sort of incident at a company called Duroc Petrochemicals on the mainland. It had shut the plant down—they obviously didn't know what they were doing! He smiled to himself and as he turned the page, he saw the headline:

SCOTTISH DRUGS DEATH SHOCK

There had been a big surge in drug-related deaths in the last 12 months. A police spokesman claimed that the cause of the problem was a big rise in drugs hitting the streets. The snag was that no one could find how the drugs were getting into the country. They knew roughly what was coming in through the ports and airports—and, anyway, the Customs and Excise had those covered—but the police were baffled, although they knew that the huge increase in supply was in "blow," or cocaine. It really was a bit of a blow! He read that in Scotland the amount of the drug consumed per session was more than double the global average. The company had provided drugs advice at one of the regular "toolbox" briefings and Moray recalled that it had been said that statistically nearly 10% of full-time employees were taking drugs. That could mean that somewhere on the rig probably 20 people had some sort of a drugs habit. It caused him to think—they were handling potentially dangerous oils and gases on the rig, and if anything went wrong, you couldn't just run away! He started to wonder how the drugs were getting into Scotland…

"Ready when you are, Moray."

Moray looked up. Gus MacIntosh, one of the process leading hands stood in the control room doorway. "I'll follow you in a minute," replied Moray. "Why don't you go and start checking the new cargo? There's a list on the control desk."

MacIntosh grabbed the clipboard containing the cargo list and left. With a final passing thought about the drugs article in the paper, Moray finished his cup of coffee, tossed the paper aside and headed back up to the main deck to help Gus with the checks and see what had been delivered.

As he reached the main deck, he saw a shadowy figure crouched over one of the crates with a wrecking bar in his hand. Something wasn't right. He couldn't tell who it was. He shouted out, but it was impossible to be heard amid the drone of machinery. Gus was ahead of him and must have disturbed the clandestine figure, because it suddenly disappeared from sight, behind the mountain of new crates and containers. Moray was determined to see what had interested the mysterious figure, because he most certainly hadn't been doing any planned work. Moray could see the crate wood was broken and splintered and he hurried to get to it. As he rushed across the deck grating, he glanced up towards the crane. A large crate was dangling on the end of the crane. It was just above Gus.

"Look out!!" he yelled. Gus looked up, just in time to see the fully loaded crate on the crane hook falling straight towards him. His hard hat fell off as he threw himself sideways in amongst the jumble of crates. The suspended crate continued with its break-neck descent and split like a rotten melon as it hit the deck, spilling metal flanges, pipe fittings and a medley of engineering spares in all directions. Everything went black for Gus as his head thumped into the metal-reinforced corner of the nearest crate.

Moray grabbed for his radio. "Man down on the production main deck! Urgent! First Aiders required!" The tannoy replicated the message calling for first aid help on the main deck. As Moray rushed over to the prone figure of Gus, he glanced up at the crane cab, but the sun was catching on the window glass and so he couldn't see the driver. What he did notice was that the crane hook was still attached to the lifting strops—clearly the crate hadn't fallen off the hook. He thought *that was odd*.

Orange-clad figures appeared from all directions. One man with a green hat with a white cross and a green grab bag knelt beside the unconscious Gus. He was bandaging the wound on Gus's head. Two others laid a stretcher board in the congested space between the jumble of crates. "We need to get him into the medical room," said one.

"Looks like a MedEvac," said the other.

Moray's radio crackled into life. "What's happened, Moray?" demanded the installation manager.

"Gus was trying to avoid a falling load and hit his head on another crate."

"Why was there a falling load?"

"Dunno yet. Looks like the crane cable brake failed."

"Get the crane isolated and barrier it off for an investigation."

"Okay—once the first aiders have got Gus to the medical room. Oh, and we may need a MedEvac chopper. Get one on standby."

As soon as Gus was stretchered off to the medical room, Moray headed for the cat ladder up to the crane. He reached the crane cab slightly out of breath. He told himself that he was out of condition. The cab was empty. No driver. He stretched across in the cramped space and felt the rather tatty seat cushion. It was warm. The driver had either gone to report the incident, or else he'd done a runner.

Moray sat in the seat and operated the joystick to raise the hook. The brake clanged as it released and the drive whirred as the hook steadily rose at a controlled rate. He released the stick and the brake motor slammed to a halt. He lowered the hook again. Not exactly a scientific study, but there didn't seem to be much wrong with the hoist! It would need the engineers to check out whether the brakes were slipping. He climbed down the ladder and asked one of the operators to rope off the area under the crane until they had properly investigated what had happened. He told the operator to isolate the power to the crane until the engineers had checked the hoist brakes.

As he walked across the deck, Moray's radio clattered. It was the installation manager again. His name was Jason Suínos, but they all knew him as "the IM." A meeting was being called in the accommodation block canteen to discuss what had just happened. Moray headed over the bridge to the accommodation platform. As he crossed the water, he heard the beat of a Sikorsky coming in to land on the helideck. As he looked up, the chopper hovered over the pad and with the precision of a surgeon, gently dropped onto the centre of the "H" symbol. The roar of the big General Electric twin engines died as the rotors idled. The passenger door slid open and six figures clambered out, ducking their heads as they carefully moved across the deck in a crouching position. Moray recognised the last three—the "Drifters" had arrived.

Moray stepped into the compact but functional canteen. The smell of beef stew wafted across the room, making him feel hungry. With the exception of the cinema room, it was the largest space on the rig and often doubled as a meeting room. The IM was there with half a dozen others. Moray nodded to the safety officer and noticed that the "A"-shift crane driver was already there.

The IM began. "The purpose of this meeting is to establish what went wrong this afternoon on the production main deck. It is not to allocate blame, but to prevent another similar incident happening. However—first—how is Gus?"

One of the first aid team, called Mairi, reported that Gus was in the medical room and had regained consciousness. However, he had a bad gash on his forehead and should be seen by professional medics as a precaution, she said.

Moray commented, "The 4 o'clock chopper has just landed. Maybe Gus could go ashore on that." The IM agreed and asked one of the operators to hold the chopper and warn the medical room. The conversation turned to the events of the afternoon. The IM asked the crane driver, Jim, what had happened.

"I've no idea!" Jim said. "I'd just finished offloading the supplies from the support vessel. It had taken about four hours and so I came down here for a cuppa."

"So, it wasn't you driving the crane?" asked the IM.

"Sally the canteen chef will vouch that I've been down here in the canteen for the last half hour. And, what's more, there were nowt wrong with the crane hoist this morning!"

Duroc

There were supposed to be two qualified crane drivers, but Jim had been the only qualified driver on the rig, until the second driver, Mark, arrived. Mark was one of the new arrivals who'd come in on the 4 o'clock chopper.

Tony, the safety officer, asked for the engineers to check over the crane hoist brake and commented that, as it appeared to be a lifting equipment failure, Ashe, the regulator, needed to be told.

The IM instructed the rig engineer to urgently arrange a check on the crane and told Tony to notify Ashe. He turned to Moray and said:

"Once the Drifters are settled into the accommodation block, get them to check out their equipment as we need to launch one of the pigs in the morning, as there's a change of spec coming on USP1"

And with that the meeting disbanded, leaving Moray to cherish the delicate aroma of boeuf bourguignon.

Chapter 5

Bluey twiddled the Rubik's cube. Whatever he did, he couldn't get the last line of white squares to complete a full side of whites. It was so frustrating. In despair, he tossed the cube into his desk drawer, took a sip of machine-produced coffee, and watched as Caitlin stalked into the office in her sexy motor cycle leathers to start another day's work. She felt that she was under scrutiny, the only woman in a male-dominated office. It was tough enough being accepted in the office, but much tougher to get accepted out in the industrial world. Many hard-nosed business managers didn't take female health and safety inspectors seriously. She was determined to make a good impression, and Bluey was a good and understanding mentor.

They exchanged trivial news, Bluey talking about what Debbie and the boys had been doing and Caitlin talking about last night at the Falkirk Town Hall where she had been to see her favourite pop group in concert. After a few minutes they both turned to their computer screens. As usual, Caitlin checked the system for any communications from the Contact Centre to see if there had been any fatalities or serious incidents overnight.

"There's one here, Bluey," she said. "On the Gannett Gamma rig. Looks like they've had a crane lifting failure." She read on. "Seems they dropped a crate and nearly hit an operator. The operator was helicoptered to the Royal Infirmary in Aberdeen

Duroc

with concussion. Seems he hit his head on a crate trying to avoid the falling load."

"OK, I'll take a look." Bluey brought the brief report up onto his screen. The information was very concise, although he noted that they had not yet identified the cause of the failure. He reached for the rolodex and spun it to the letter "G." He looked for the number for the safety officer on the Gannet Gamma rig. Nothing there. He couldn't even remember a name. He called the switchboard to ask to be put through to whoever oversaw health and safety there.

"Duroc Offshore," was the telephonist's reply. Bluey paused. He had completely forgotten that Duroc also had North Sea interests. Was it a coincidence that Duroc had reported two incidents in the last few days?

"Can I speak to the health and safety officer on Gannet Gamma, please?"

"Hold the line, I'll see if I can connect you... Sorry, sir, no one is answering. Can anyone else help?"

"What about the installation manager?"

The IM answered with a polite European accent but was not very forthcoming. Apparently, an investigation was underway, but the root cause of the crane failure had not yet been identified. Bluey had asked about the condition of Gus MacIntosh. The IM confirmed that Gus was in the Aberdeen Royal Infirmary and although he was shaken up and had a bad head-ache, there was no long-term damage. He should be home after a couple of days of "observation." Bluey thought Gus had been lucky and that it could so easily have been fatal. An idea flashed through his mind: was this incident intended as some sort of warning? The fact that the rig was operated by Duroc gave him a hunch that it might be time to make a visit. He had completed his helicopter survival training at one of the establishments in Aberdeen over a year before and, despite several trips to other

North Sea rigs, happily he had never had to put the training into practice! However, he would not be able to take Caitlin with him as she hadn't yet done the survival training. Perhaps it would be a good time to get her trained up in case she ever needed to go off-shore.

Caitlin was really enthusiastic about the possibility of being paid for spending a few days in a swimming pool. It apparently hadn't occurred to her that it would be hard work and even a bit scary. She was very sporty and so the idea of survival training didn't faze her at all. It was all part of the rich tapestry of life. She agreed without a second thought.

Bluey told Caitlin that he planned to go out to the Gannet Gamma to try and understand what had gone wrong. He asked her to continue to follow up on the incident at Duroc Petrochemicals and, in particular, to interview Carl Dunne again. Something didn't add up. He shared with her his concern that it seemed too much of a co-incidence that there had been a potentially fatal incident at Duroc Petrochemicals and now another one at Gannet Gamma—and both were owned by Duroc. He asked her to look out for any evidence of a link between the two events.

*****

Caitlin felt elated. Bluey was trusting her to carry out the rest of the investigation at Duroc Petrochemicals on her own. It was the first time. She had to admit that her elation was mixed with a little anxiety, but she would cope. She had been born under Aries—"Survive and thrive!" Bluey had left to drive up to Dyce Airport by Aberdeen yesterday afternoon and now things were down to her. She was on her way to meet Martyn Southwick again at Duroc, and her main task was to re-interview Carl Dunne. It was likely to be in the Scots vernacular and therefore hard work. But she could take the Triumph Tiger as compensation.

Martyn Southwick was an easy person to deal with. He understood the need to get to the root cause of the bellows failure, but the plant was still shut down and Brodric Reynolds, the plant manager, was still on the warpath. Carl Dunne was waiting with his union representative in a small conference room in the admin building. Caitlin thanked him for making himself available and apologised for having to have a further discussion. However, she reminded him that he was still under caution.

"Carl, can you tell me who it was who asked you to inspect the bellows?" She expected a "No comment" response, but Carl obviously had other ideas.

"Ah dinnae ken. Ah wis workin' oan isolating th' boiler feed treatment system. Th' plant wis bein' stairted up whin ah git a phane message that th' turbine belluws wantit inspection afore we stairted up. Ah asked whit th' inspection wis keekin fur. A' he said wis that ah hud served mah time 'n' ah shuid ken. Then he rang aff."

"Who was it that you took the phone call from?"

"He didnae say. Bit he tellt me tae tak' as lang as ah wantit tae dae th' jab. He sounded insistent, lik' yin o' th' bosses."

"Was it Brodric Reynolds?"

Dunne hesitated "Na, ah dinnae think sae. Bit a've heard th' voice afore." He was an accomplished liar.

"Where did you hear it?"

Dunne hesitated again. "Ah used tae wirk oan th' North Sea oil rigs. Ah mind that voice thare."

"Was it a man or a woman's voice?"

"Man. 'Twas definetly a man's voice."

Caitlin thanked Carl for the information and asked him to let her know if he remembered the name of the caller. As they left the room, Martyn turned to her and suggested that she should have a chat with the production controller. As the job title suggested, the production controller was responsible for planning and managing the arrangements for production. Martyn suggested that she concentrate on understanding the raw materials situation.

Bluey had asked Caitlin to call him each evening that he was away to give him an update about the bellows incident at Duroc Petrochemicals. During their first evening phone call, she told Bluey how Carl Dunne claimed that he had been told over the phone to drop everything and inspect the turbine bellows. He'd said the voice was familiar, but he couldn't remember exactly who it was. However, there might be a link to the North Sea rigs. She then described the conversation with the Duroc production controller. He'd been very forthcoming. It seemed that the gas feedstock levels had been critically low for some time. It wasn't clear if they had run out of funds or whether the North Sea pipeline was restricting flows. Either way, as Iain, the plant engineer had hinted during the earlier meeting with Brodric Reynolds, gas feedstock levels were definitely critically low. On the day of the boiler feedwater pump failure, the levels had been so low that the plant would have had to shut down anyway for lack of feed. After the pump was repaired, feedstock flows from the North Sea had started again and then suddenly stopped, so there was still not enough feed to re-start the plant with steady production. Caitlin mentioned that she had not been able to find a permit to work for the bellows job. This was an essential document that ensured that all the necessary safety precautions had been carried out before work commenced. In normal circumstances it would be a dismissible offence to do work on the bellows without the required safety checks being carried out. It was clear from plant records that the bellows inspection was not a regular job, and that Carl Dunne had never done it before. The question was, did Dunne understand the critical importance of the support rings? Or had he left one out intentionally? Caitlin felt that the phone call that Carl had received to divert him to the bellows job must have come from someone who carried some authority and who was known to him. Both the Ashe inspectors initially suspected Brodric Reynolds, but Dunne had specifically excluded him. Metallurgical tests carried out by Iain, the plant engineer, had confirmed that there was nothing wrong with the bellows material. It looked as though the immediate cause of the failure was the fact that Dunne had not replaced one of the support rings. Caitlin would talk to the bellows manufacturers tomorrow and continue to try and identify Carl Dunne's caller.

*****

On Gannet Gamma, the three Drifters were inspecting the equipment that had been unloaded from the support vessel the previous day. Their equipment was too heavy to transport by chopper and so it was always shipped in. Two large wooden crates were on the production deck. The crates were clearly identified by black stencilled lettering announcing:

SCOTTISH PIPELINE SERVICES
—RADIO ACTIVITY—DO NOT OPEN

"Moura's not going to like this!" said the unshaven one, pointing to where the crate had been broken open. "Never mind that—let's get the gear out and see if anything is missing," said the taller one.

Moray strolled over to chat with them. He spoke to the team leader. "Hi, Stylo. The crane is out of action after an incident, but we still need the USP1 pipeline to be pigged in the morning. You'll need to rig up lifting gear to get your kit down to the pigging station. I can send you a couple of extra guys if you need them."

The Drifters looked anxiously at each other.

"No need, we can manage, if you can lend us the lifting gear," replied Stylo quickly. "We'll need a permit to load the pig this evening and then another to launch it in the morning." Moray agreed and got on the radio to arrange lifting tackle from the engineering store and then left them to their own devices, whilst he sorted out the permits.

The tall one, called Lanky, set to opening the damaged crates, whilst the unshaven one and Stylo went to set up the lifting gear. The pigging station was below the main deck and was equipped with a lifting beam for loading the pigs. The problem was that all the equipment had to be lowered down from the production deck. The two Drifters found a suitable beam from which they could mount the lifting gear, and whilst the unshaven one finished lashing it in place, Stylo went back to see if Lanky had finished opening the damaged crate.

Lanky indicated that the equipment all seemed to be in place and undamaged. "There was no need for Maclean to panic and try and scare someone off with the crane after all." "Maclean" was the code name for their undercover contact on the rig. He gesticulated towards the open crates. They had started using a novel new type of "intelligent" pig, which would not only separate the products by the use of flexible rubber-like cups—not unlike toilet plungers—at each end, but it also had the ability to continuously measure the thickness of the pipeline using ultrasonic detection. The ultrasonic detector was still under development and therefore rather large, and so it was housed in a cylindrical stainless-steel canister located between the two sets of pig cups. Stylo inspected the pig. There was no sign of damage to either the cups or the canister. Moura would be pleased to know that. He and Lanky levered the pig onto a small trolley and wheeled it across the deck to where the unshaven one had set up the lifting tackle. Using a webbing strop, they carefully lifted the pig from the trolley and onto the deck below. True to his word, Moray had provided a permit for them to load the pig into the trap at the pigging station.

The problem with pigging was that if anything went wrong, all you knew was that it hadn't turned up at the other end! This could be a nightmare on a long undersea pipeline, because you just didn't know where the pig was stuck. To ease the problem of retrieving the stuck pig, the Drifters usually put a very low-dose radioisotope on the pig so that, if necessary, divers could detect its position using a Geiger counter.

Stylo sent the other two Drifters to collect the isotope in its heavy lead protective container from the opened crates. They returned several minutes later, straining to carry a cylindrical metal case with a yellow and black radiation warning sign on its side. Stylo donned his radiation protection, put up the warning signs and sent the other two away whilst he loaded the isotope tracer. He had already removed the ultrasonic detection device covers in order to insert the radioisotope tracer. He took out a small pen torch from his overalls pocket and looked carefully inside the stainless-steel canister.

He smiled to himself. There was no sign of the revolutionary ultrasonic detection equipment!

He closed the canister and declared to himself, "All ready for launching tomorrow!" Moura would be pleased.

*****

It was 8 a.m. the following morning, and as usual it was raining. The Drifters had their permit to launch the pig. Stylo and Lanky had rigged up the lifting gear and prepared to hoist it into the trap, ready for launching. Lanky was a bit too eager, causing the pig to tilt at one end. It was caught on a piece of protruding metal and seemed to be stuck. Stylo yelled at him to pull on the chains to free the pig. The pig body was wet with rain and as he pulled at the chains, the chains slipped and the pig crashed to the deck, narrowly missing Lanky's leg. Stylo was furious. He sprang over to the pig, which was lying on the grating, and examined it caressingly. Luckily there was no serious damage. He chided Lanky, "You were lucky there—Moura would have had your guts for garters if the consignment had been damaged!"

No concern for my wellbeing, then, thought Lanky. Ten minutes later the pig was safely in the trap. Stylo swung the large door on the trap closed and spun the eight big wing nuts, sealing the pig into the USP pipeline that went to the shore. After a short radio call to the control room to get authorisation to launch, Stylo carefully opened the valves that sent the pig on its way. The indicator on top of the trap flipped over, showing that the pig was gone.

Chapter 6

Bluey strolled into the departure hall at Aberdeen's Dyce Airport and headed for the helicopter flight check-in desks. His flight to the Gannet Gamma rig was on time. He wandered through the duty-free sales area, half-heartedly looking for a gift for Debbie. He selected and paid for a small bottle of "Attar Rose," before he properly read the label. There would be consequences for suggesting that his wife needed a bottle of deodorant!

There was no time to take the mistaken gift back, as Bluey's flight was boarding. He joined the small group of 15 oilrig workers shambling out to the awaiting helicopter. He climbed aboard and took a single seat beside one of the small windows. No sooner had he fastened his belt and donned his ear defenders, than the twin jet engines roared into life. The pilot was chattering away into his helmet microphone and as he pulled up on the collective, the S-92 floated up into the air, the nose dipped into a left-hand turn and they were on their way.

Bluey gazed nonchalantly out of the window, trying to identify landmarks, but they quickly crossed the coastline and there was nothing but grey sea below. Bluey turned his attention to the Rubik's cube in his coat pocket. The helicopter was cruising at an altitude of 12,000 feet, doing 175 miles per hour. It would take about 40 minutes to reach the rig.

The flight was largely uneventful and it seemed to take no time at all before the helicopter lost height and was starting to circle around a rig installation. It was made up of three different platforms linked by gantries. Bluey could see that the big box-like structure on the southernmost module had the words "GANNET GAMMA" painted in huge letters on the side. Above that was a helipad. That would be the accommodation module. Bluey looked over at the other two platforms. The northernmost structure had a large gantry sticking up. Bluey guessed that was the derrick on the drilling module. The centre module also had a type of derrick sticking out at a weird angle. *That must be the production platform*, he thought.

The pilot cut the speed of the S-92 down almost to a crawl as the aircraft approached the helipad. Bluey could see all the details of the production platform. He could see the crane that he had come to investigate at the corner of the module. It obviously wasn't working at the moment. He realised that the derrick that he had noticed sticking out of the side of the production platform was actually a flarestack, to safely dispose of and burn excess gas, when either it was not needed or when a safety relief valve lifted. Bluey could see right down the flarestack. He had never seen one from this angle before. It was amazing.

Suddenly the helicopter seemed to be engulfed in an orange cloud of searing heat. The cabin was instantly full of profanities. It was like flying through hell. The outer glass of the window was cracking. The engines roared to a crescendo as the pilot put on full throttle to try and lift the machine away from the rig, but it was falling. Bluey, along with the other occupants of the cabin, was struggling to put on his life jacket. There was just not enough space in the small cabin. Bluey glanced out of the window. The helicopter had dropped down and was almost skimming across the sea surface. They were below the flames now but could see the legs of the rigs to their left. Everything seemed to be in slow motion. The cabin chatter had gone quiet and 16 pale faces were staring anxiously out of the partially shattered and sooty windows at the sea just a few metres below them. If the engines faltered now, they were done for.

Bluey glanced at the blackened fuel tank outside the cabin, just below the window. It was heavily charred. It was designed to be crash-resistant, but what if it was subjected to a flamethrower? Had the designers thought of that? The chopper was moving away from the rig, but it had no height. Bluey could see oil rig workers swarming around the lifeboat stations. A bright orange lifeboat, which appeared to be almost standing on its bow end, suddenly shot down its metal slipway from the accommodation platform and burst onto the water with a huge splash, almost submerging for a moment. As soon as the spray subsided, the lifeboat was bobbing on the surface and starting to pull away from the rig, heading towards the helicopter.

On the flight deck, the co-pilot was sending out distress messages whilst his colleague was wrestling to keep the machine airborne. They were flying away from the rig to keep clear of the flames, but if they were going to ditch in the sea, they needed to be near lifeboats. They couldn't see that behind them a lifeboat was already in the water. The pilot announced out loud that he was going to hover the aircraft and turn to face the rig. He controlled the tail rotor with his pedals and swung the chopper around to face the rig, which was now over a mile away. Orange plumes of flame were belching out of the flarestack on the middle module. "We flew through the flare!" he announced to his colleague. He pulled back on the cyclic control, which cut down the forward speed. He then pulled up on the collective, which should have lifted the aircraft. But it didn't. Hovering this close to the water left a disc on the surface of the sea, but, at the edge of the disc, spray was being thrown up by the wash of the main rotor, almost obscuring the brightly coloured helicopter from view.

From the rig, Moray Stewart leaned on the handrails and watched the Sikorsky skimming above the water. "He's in trouble—he can't get any height," he murmured. "Looks like he's going to ditch!" He spoke into his radio and called for another lifeboat to be prepared for launching. Just then his radio barked back with a message from one of the mechanical technicians, reporting that the pressure safety relief valve had lifted on the gas compressor. Moray realised immediately that that had been the cause of the sudden flare that had caused the problem for the chopper. He rushed back to the production module compressor deck and found some of the maintenance crew huddled around the compressor. The noise was unbearable. It sounded as if the full discharge of the compressor was being diverted through the relief valve, and going directly to the flarestack. Moray hit the red mushroom-topped emergency stop and the compressor began to coast to a standstill. The noise was still deafening but Moray knew it would take some time for the USP pipeline pressure to drop. He looked at the flare and thought that the size of the flame was starting to diminish. After a quick message to the control room to explain what he had done, he started to muse over what could have caused this sudden increase in the pipeline pressure. It was most unusual.

Back on the chopper, Bluey thought that he could see a bright orange boat heading towards them through the spray.

"Prepare to ditch! Prepare to ditch!" came the pilot's voice over the cabin intercom. The passengers looked at each other. They had all done their HUET (Helicopter Underwater Escape Training) but none had ever put it into practice. Bluey noticed that a big guy in the single rear seat seemed to be sobbing to himself. He called out for everyone to have their rebreathing devices ready—this would give them a little longer underwater before they ran out of air. It might not help, but it gave everyone something to focus their attention on rather than thinking about what was about to happen. The helicopter was struggling to keep level. The left-hand wheel and fuel sponson were already almost in the water.

They were almost stationary, just half a mile from the rig, and the lifeboat was getting closer. Suddenly the cabin lurched sideways as a strong gust caught the chopper. The left-hand landing wheel dropped into the water, dragging the helicopter to a greater angle. The main rotor caught a wave, smashing a blade in a flurry of water. The rotor continued to thrash but was now out of balance, with only two of the four blades intact, causing the fuselage of the machine to suddenly leap up and throw the helicopter upside down, into the path of the oncoming lifeboat.

It was chaos in the upturned chopper cabin. Some passengers were hanging upside down in their seat belts, but those who had released their belts in preparation for evacuation in ditching, were being tossed around as if in a washing machine. The height of the cabin was less than two metres, and water was already surging in through shattered windows and flooding the upturned ceiling. The helicopter was sinking fast. Then the lights went out.

It took Bluey a moment to understand what was going on. It was deadly quiet. He was suspended upside down in his seat with his head in rapidly rising water. Debris was floating everywhere. In the half light from the small windows, he found the seat belt buckle, but his weight was preventing him from opening it. He pulled himself up towards the chair and the belt buckle suddenly pinged open; then he fell head first onto the ceiling and another crumpled body. He got himself the right way up and looked around. He could see that there were several bodies against the inverted cockpit bulkhead. Those passengers obviously hadn't had their seat belts fastened. His neighbour across the S-92's aisle was still hanging upside down in his seat. Bluey helped him release his buckle and he fell to the ceiling. Bluey dragged his head above the water but he was OK.

The water was now waist-deep. Bluey waded towards the cockpit and the bodies against the cockpit wall. There was a lot of blood and he prepared himself for some gruesome scenes. It was lucky that the light was so poor! The first victim was a crumpled and still heap. Bluey felt for a pulse. Nothing there. The other two were still breathing. One had head injuries and was mumbling incoherently, but the other seemed to just be badly shaken up. Bluey slapped his face. "Come on, you've got to get out!" This seemed to do the trick. Bluey suggested that they help the other injured man to the escape hatch, and so they manhandled him to the main door, which was still above water and jammed partially open. There was a queue of dishevelled and wet bodies at the door waiting to get out. *Typical*, thought Bluey. *It's only in Britain that you would find people forming a queue to get out of a crashed helicopter!* The water was now at chin level. It wouldn't be long before the chopper went down. He was still clutching his rebreather bag. He put in the mouthpiece, ready to put the bag in place, and he noticed that the guy helping him with the injured man did the same. Something floating on the water bumped against his cheek. It was a Rubik's cube. He grabbed it and thrust it under the water into his pocket.

Some of the oil workers were already squatting on the outside of the S-92's upturned fuselage. Bluey could see out, but was irritated by the fact that the workers outside weren't already getting into the lifeboat. He called for people to move over so that he and the others could get out. They pushed their injured colleague up through the door, where he was welcomed by a flurry of willing hands. The water was now into the doorway and Bluey fixed his rebreather bag and then tried to drag himself outside. There was very little space, but strong hands were pulling him through. The daylight temporarily blinded him, but he could feel that the space was very congested. "Where's the lifeboat?" he called.

"It's over there, mate!" said a voice. An arm was wafted over the sea. As Bluey's day vision returned, he could make out a bright orange pyramid bobbing no more than 20 metres from the wrecked chopper. It didn't look like the lifeboat he had seen racing towards them when the chopper had been about to ditch. "What happened?" he said.

"Looks like the rotors caught the bow of the lifeboat and cut through the buoyancy chambers," came the reply. Basically, the lifeboat was on end and 80% of it was under water. It was being kept afloat by air trapped in the stern. Bizarrely, the propeller on the stern was still spinning with an eerie scream. Bluey thought of Murphy's Law: "If anything can go wrong, it will!" Just then, two helmet-clad figures swam around the wreck and Bluey realised that the two pilots had managed to escape through the cockpit windscreens. Although they were very wet and cold, the pilots had selflessly chosen to stay in the water, as the congested wreck was already on the point of sinking below the waves.

Bluey thought that the monotonous scream of the lifeboat's exposed propeller was changing, until he realised that it was being supplemented by another, deeper sound. It was the sound of another propeller, but this one was in the water, and it was driving a second lifeboat towards the wrecks. Much of the fuselage of the S-92 was already underwater. The survivors were sitting or lying on the outside of the cabin and it was already largely submerged. There was a half-hearted cheer as the clockwork orange of the second lifeboat hove into view. The

Simon W. Pain

lifeboat was designed to get people away from the rig quickly, rather than to pluck people out of the sea, and so the process of boarding was frustratingly slow. Bluey was one of the last to be hauled aboard, after helping get the man with head injuries aboard as well as the pilot and co-pilot. As Bluey gazed out of the windows of the lifeboat, his teeth chattering, one of the oil worker crew on the lifeboat asked him how he was, and provided him with a thick warm blanket from one of the stowage lockers, along with a steaming mug of cocoa. Cocooned in blankets, he slowly started to warm up and he noticed a third lifeboat heading out from the rig. As they passed it on the way back to the rig, he saw it contained a team of frogmen who were obviously going to search for survivors of the wrecked lifeboat. As he turned to look out to sea, he noticed that the wreck of the Sikorsky was nowhere to be seen.

Chapter 7

Caitlin was making her daily evening phone call to Bluey to report on progress at Duroc Petrochemicals. When the call eventually got connected to Bluey on the rig, he told her about his in-flight incident. Bluey tried to downplay how serious it had been, but Caitlin was perceptive and soon realised that it was much more serious than he was letting on.

Bluey explained that the helicopter had been hit by an unplanned flare which seemed to affect the helicopter's control systems, and they had been forced to ditch. Caitlin asked if he was OK, as it all sounded pretty scary. Bluey told her that he was still in one piece, but some people hadn't made it. He reckoned that there'd been 15 passengers and two crewmen on board. He thought that only 14 of the 17 had got out alive; one of those had serious head injuries and several others had minor injuries. He went on to say that a lifeboat had also been lost when it was struck by the helicopter rotor, and he thought that there had been no survivors. He warned her that it was likely to be reported in the media once information got out.

Bluey explained that he would have to stay out on the rig for much longer than he had expected, as this event would need some detailed investigation. Although the Marine Investigation Branch would investigate the chopper and lifeboat accidents and associated fatalities, Ashe would need to find out why there had been a sudden flare, as that had possibly been the initial cause of the helicopter crash. Bluey told Caitlin that he would have to rely on her to complete the investigation of the bellows incident at Duroc Petrochemicals.

Caitlin told Bluey that the main cause of the Duroc bellows failure was still not clear. She had a feeling that the inspection of the bellows was a set-up, but so far she didn't know why. The bellows failure looked as though it was due to a lack of understanding of the importance of the support rings. Clearly, Carl Dunne had never done that job before, and although he was a trained and experienced technician, he didn't understand the important part that the rings played in the performance of the bellows. Not only that, he had not been given any clear guidance on what the purpose of the inspection was. She was confident that Iain, the engineer, understood the design and construction of the bellows, but that he had not been involved in any way with the last-minute decision to do the inspection. That made it very odd—that someone else would request a check on such a piece of equipment. Iain would normally be the person who issued orders for maintenance tasks, unless it was a breakdown. Caitlin suggested to Bluey that while the inspection of the bellows had been intentional, the explosive failure had not been intended, and had arisen from lack of knowledge and bad luck.

"Have you had any luck finding who ordered Carl to inspect the bellows?" asked Bluey.

Caitlin replied that they were no further forward on that, although Iain was trying to find out.

"What about the plant—has it started up yet?"

"The controller mentioned this afternoon that the feedstock tanks are starting to fill up," Caitlin replied. "But there was another sudden interruption of the gas supply today. It was almost as if the gas supply had been isolated without any notice.

Duroc

The pressure in the line is now almost zero. So, the plant is still shutdown and Brodric Reynolds is almost apoplectic!"

"That's funny," said Bluey. It sounded as though he was amused at the thought of Reynolds being apoplectic! "I'm pretty sure that the gas is fed through the USP1 pipeline from Gannet Gamma. That's why they bought Duroc Petrochemicals—so that they would have a captive, wholly-owned customer for the gas."

"What's odd about that?"

"Well, Duroc Petrochemicals were complaining about losing their gas feedstock shortly after the helicopter was ditching in the North Sea."

"You think that they are connected?"

"Remember that the reason the chopper went down was because of a massive gas flare on the GG. It was so large that it must have been full gas production diverted from the pipeline up the flare. It was clearly unexpected, otherwise the chopper pilot would have been warned."

"You think somebody shut the pipeline valves?" Caitlin asked.

"Either that or there was one hell of a blockage!" said Bluey. "See what else you can find out about how long the USP gas pipeline will be shut down for."

Bluey warned Caitlin that as he would be on the rig for some time, he might need her to come out to relieve him, and so she had better get on and organise her HUET survival training so that she could make the trip. Caitlin pulled a face. The training suddenly didn't seem quite so exciting now that she knew that Bluey's helicopter had gone down.

Just before the call ended Caitlin added an afterthought. "By the way, Iain said the pig never arrived!"

"That's it!" said Bluey. "They've got the pig stuck! That must have been what caused the blockage in the pipe. And that caused the massive flare that took out the helicopter!"

Simon W. Pain

Bluey rang off and contacted Debbie and his boss to update them on the day's events before they were seen on the TV news. He warned an alarmed Debbie that his trip was going to be extended for several days. He sent his love to her and the boys, and told them not to worry—that he was fine.

*****

During the late afternoon and evening the helipad was like a terminal at Heathrow with rescue and medevac choppers coming in and out, taking the injured back to Aberdeen. One red and white rescue helicopter was still hovering over the wreck of the first lifeboat. The third lifeboat was still on the scene and a rig support vessel was coming into view, clearly summoned to assist with the recovery of the wrecks.

Jason, the installation manager, had called a meeting in the accommodation block canteen to discuss what had happened that afternoon. He wanted to get feedback whilst things were still fresh in people's minds.

"This meeting is just to establish the facts as we know them," said Jason. "I have asked Steve Craythorn, whom some of you know—he was the pilot of the S-92—to join us, and also we have Bluey Scrimshaw from Ashe, who was a passenger on the flight. He was visiting the GG to investigate the recent crane failure. I hope that we will give them both our full cooperation."

Jason asked initially for a summary of the consequences of the accident. It appeared that both the Sikorsky and the first lifeboat had been lost in the incident. Moray, the production supervisor, said that the crew of four in the lifeboat were all unaccounted for. Pilot Craythorn confirmed that there had been two crew members and 15 passengers on the flight. Moray confirmed that 14 people from the helicopter crash had been rescued and brought to the rig. One of those was seriously injured and had already been medevac'd to Aberdeen with serious head injuries. Three other casualties had also been airlifted back to the mainland. The bodies of the lifeboat crew had been found, but the three missing passengers from the chopper had not been recovered yet.

Jason asked the pilot to explain what he recalled of the event. After describing the fact that the helicopter had flown through the flare, Steve Craythorn recounted that vertical control of the aircraft had been lost. Between sobs he recalled how he hadn't been able to maintain height and he'd taken the decision to ditch. That should have been quite straightforward, but at the last minute a strong gust of wind had caught the chopper and flipped it over. The broken rotors had caught the lifeboat as it approached. After that he hadn't seen what happened to the lifeboat. The helicopter had sunk in less than ten minutes. The two pilots had escaped out of the shattered windscreens.

Jason turned to Bluey and asked him what he recalled.

"We were coming in to land and approaching from the west side of the installation," said Bluey. "We were almost in a hover as we passed the middle platform where the flarestack is. As we passed over the end of the flarestack, I could look down the stack, and except for the pilot lights it appeared to be empty. With no warning, suddenly the chopper was engulfed in flame. I couldn't see where it was coming from, but I assumed that gas had discharged from the tip of the flare and been ignited by the pilot lights. This assumption was confirmed because when the chopper turned back towards the rig, just before it crashed, I could see a large flare from the flarestack. The key question for me is why was there such a sudden, large flare from the rig?"

"That indeed is one question!" confirmed Jason. "The other is - why was the chopper so close to the flarestack?" He went on to say, "Moray, what do we know about the cause of the flare?"

Moray Stewart confirmed that the discharge gas compressor safety relief valve had lifted and that, as a result, the full pipeline flow had discharged up the flare. Moray himself had immediately shut down the compressor and isolated the pipeline, but he was unsure why the relief valve had lifted.

Bluey suggested that the relief valve should be examined to see if it was faulty, but, if not, then more gas had been trying to enter the pipeline than was being used.

The meeting then snowballed into uncontrolled discussion of what could have caused the sudden flare. The general opinion was that something must have caused the flow of gas to stop in the pipeline. It was suggested that this could have been some major impact with the pipe. Someone suggested that the sinking helicopter could have hit the pipe—that was until Jason pointed out that the flare had been the *cause* of the helicopter crash and so the pipeline blockage had happened prior to the sinking of the chopper! There was a suggestion that perhaps a ship had collided with the pipe, but unless it had been close to shore, that was unlikely because of the depth of the pipe, and there had been no distress calls from sinking ships in the area. Jason asked Moray whether it was possible that an internal part of a valve could have fallen off and blocked the flow, but Moray had checked the valves at the rig end of the pipeline and they were all functioning OK.

Bluey spoke up. "What about a pig?"

Jason looked at him with surprise. "What *about* a pig?" he queried.

"I understand that you are undergoing a specification change on the gas and that you have launched a pig."

"How do you know that?" demanded Jason.

"It's my job to know," Bluey said with a smile. "Perhaps a pig is stuck in the line?" He paused. "Has anyone checked to see if the pig arrived at Duroc Petrochemicals?"

Duroc

Jason looked embarrassed and told Moray to go and check the status of the pig. Whilst Moray was gone, they speculated on what to do if the pig was stuck. It seemed that it had never happened before, and so no one was quite sure how they would find it in over 100 miles of pipe. Stylo, from Scottish Pipeline Services, spoke up to say that they had put a low-dose radioactive tracer on the pig, and so, if it was stuck, they should be able to find it. Someone suggested that 100 miles would be an awfully long swim for a diver with a Geiger counter!

It took Moray less than five minutes to return pale-faced to the canteen with the news that the pig had never arrived at the Duroc Petrochemicals plant. Stylo's face was a picture.

Jason was clearly not amused by the news. "How the hell can the pig be stuck?"

Stylo rattled off a series of defences, but it really was academic. The pig was stuck and that was all there was to it. The question was, could the pig be freed off, or was it a case of finding it? Either way, gas flows to the mainland were likely to be interrupted for some time. The discussion shifted to finding ways of moving the pig. Stylo suggested sending another pig to try and chase out the offender. Moray pointed out that the stuck pig was preventing gas flowing down the pipe—hence the sudden major flare. If gas couldn't flow down the pipe, then another pig would have nothing to propel it along. Not only that, but if a second pig got stuck, they would have double the problem.

Jason agreed. He looked to Bluey and asked what he thought. Bluey suggested that it might be possible to push the pig back to the rig pig-trap using higher gas pressure from the mainland end of the pipe.

Jason put the suggestion to the meeting and it was agreed to try pushing the pig back, if only because no one else had a better idea.

Simon W. Pain

As the meeting broke up, Bluey scanned the menu card on the canteen table. He spotted a maple-baked pork loin and apple platter. The rig chef was renowned for his sumptuous main courses and so Bluey decided to indulge himself before finding his cabin. He gave a nod to the chef and sat quietly twiddling his Rubik's cube, awaiting his feast.

*****

The phone was ringing. Brodric Reynolds leaned across his desk and scooped up the receiver. It was Moray Stewart from Gannet Gamma. It seemed they had a problem. The rig had carelessly lost a pig in the USP1 pipeline. Reynolds knew that there was some sort of a problem because the gas flows that were his raw material had stopped earlier in the afternoon. He was furious. "How the hell can you lose a pig!" he demanded.

Moray apologised profusely and explained that they wanted to try pushing the pig back using gas pressure from Duroc Petrochemicals. Reynolds had little option but to comply, but he insisted that it would be at Duroc Offshore's cost and he would be seeking further compensation, as the plant was just about to re-start after the bellows incident. He rang off.

Brodric was sitting with his head in his hands when the door opened and Iain came in. Iain listened quietly whilst the angry production manager explained why the raw materials flows had been cut and that there was now a blockage in USP1. He said that Gannet Gamma management team were asking to use gas pressure to push the pig back to the rig.

"It can't happen," Iain replied. "Where the pipeline surfaces in the storage compound, there is a large non-return valve which is intended to prevent back flow. The valve is welded into the pipeline and so, even if we could empty the pipe of gas, it would be almost impossible to remove the valve. You'd better

Duroc

get back to them and tell them that the best thing they can do is to start looking for their pig."

Chapter 8

It was nearly midnight and Bluey and the rig management team were back in the canteen. Jason had been told that Duroc Petrochemicals could not reverse the flow in the USP and so the pig would have to be found. This gave them two headaches: first, how to find the pig, and second, once the pig was found how to get it out of the pipe when the pipe was under 90 metres of water on the seabed.

Bluey suggested that they could roughly work out how far the pig had got, as they knew at what time it had been launched and what time the flaring had started, indicating when the pig got stuck. The flow rate of the gas and the time of the pig's travel could then give them a rough distance of travel along the pipe. That would be a lot better than searching over 100 miles of seabed. Greg Martin, the production unit engineer, agreed and suggested a further refinement. Apparently, the type of pigs used in the USP pipelines carried ultrasonic detection equipment which monitored the thickness of the pipe walls while travelling along to check for corrosion. He suggested looking back at the previous records to see if there was any evidence of damage to the pipeline that would stop a pig.

These two actions were agreed, and although this was encouraging it would not exactly locate the pig. Jason suggested it would need a remotely operated vehicle (ROV) using a Geiger counter to precisely locate the position. He would contact

Duroc

headquarters to see if there were any diving vessels in the vicinity. Jason left the canteen to explore the availability of support vessels and those remaining in the meeting started to speculate about what to do once the pig was found.

Greg Martin explained, "We can't just cut the pipe and take the pig out. It would be like providing a plughole in the North Sea—it might just drain out of the pipe and sink the whole east coast of Scotland! The priority is to get gas flowing again along the undersea pipeline." He suggested that this meant constructing a by-pass around the pig. Once the by-pass was installed, the gas transfer could restart and they could take their time to remove the pig—or they could just leave it there! However, constructing a bypass under 90 metres of seawater was going to be no picnic.

Bluey asked how they would undertake the repair in such a difficult environment. Greg explained that it would involve a "saturation" diving team who could spend a significant amount of time underwater, together with a specialised contractor who could provide the expertise to connect branches into the pipe to allow for the by-pass to be constructed. Both of these things were highly specialised and expensive to do. Stylo, the pigging contractor, helpfully explained that Scottish Pipeline Services could carry out the isolation of the USP pipeline if Duroc could arrange the welding required. His eyes lit up at the prospect of a very lucrative contract.

It seemed that the meeting had agreed a way forward for the by-pass, so all it needed now was to find the pig!

Bluey stopped in the canteen for a quick snack and then decided that, as there was little that he could do to help with the stuck pig, he would spend his time looking into the real reason that he was on the rig: what had caused the crane failure? The weather had deteriorated whilst they had been in the canteen. As Bluey crossed the bridge to the production module the wind and rain buffeted his face as he clung onto the handrails for dear life. If Debbie could see him now, she would realise that his was not just an office job! When he reached the main deck, it was getting dark. The beams from bright floodlights sparkled with horizontal raindrops. As he dipped his head, Bluey cursed at the thought that he was going to get a soaking again, for the second time that day.

The main deck was still a chaotic array of crates and pallets of equipment. The crane had been out of use for over 24 hours, at his request, and so nothing had been moved other than those things that were manhandleable. Yellow and black marker tape was looped around some of the crates like some sort of low-budget Christmas decoration. From the splinters of wood inside the tape barrier it seemed he had found the location where the crate had fallen. He couldn't see where the broken crates had gone. Without crossing the tapes, he walked back across the main deck looking for the damaged crate. He was about to give up when a strong gust of wind caused him to stumble onto his knees on the grating floor. He could see through the floor grating to the pigging station, and beside it he saw the remains of a damaged crate. Struggling against the wind, he lurched over to the top of the stairway and down to the pigging station on the floor below. There, beside the pig-launching equipment, was a stack of broken wood. Bluey picked up shards of the split wood. Some of it had stencilled printing on it. He already knew what the words would say. As he held the broken pieces together, he could make out the printing, which read "...ish Pipeline Serv..." The fact that Scottish Pipeline Services had left their damaged crates beside the pigging station was no great surprise and didn't point to a conclusion. But it was interesting.

He looked up, and through the grating he saw an orange-clad figure. Was he sheltering from the weather or was he looking at Bluey? The figure slipped away into the shadows and

Duroc

Bluey turned his attention back to the timber debris beside the pigging station. It would have taken more than a man with a wrecking bar to cause that damage. This could be the crate that had been dropped from the crane. In amongst the discarded crates, he saw a circular container made of bright metal, glinting in the floodlights. On the side of the cylinder was a yellow and black propeller-shaped label. The warning symbol for radioactivity.

Bluey thought back to what Stylo had said about using radioactive tracers on the pigs. He tagged the cylinder so it would be ready to take back to the mainland. It would be made of lead and too heavy to carry back to his cabin in the accommodation block, and, in any case, he didn't have any personal radiation monitoring.

It was clear that the crate that had been dropped had contained equipment for the "Drifters." After a brief study of the pigging station, Bluey retraced his steps, heading towards the staircase up to the main deck. He was aware of someone on the grating floor above him. When he stopped, so did the footsteps above. When he moved forward, the footsteps followed. He strained to see any detail through the lattice grating above his head. It was too dark to see any detail. He flashed his torch beam up through the grating, but where he had heard footsteps, there was only silence, and he couldn't see any movement. But he felt he was being followed!

He was at the base of the staircase and sprang up the stairs, taking three at a time, to try and catch sight of his stalker. The floodlights shone brightly on the main deck, but the deck was festooned with crates awaiting storage and they cast low-level shadows all around the deck. If anyone was there, they would be hiding in the shadows now. Bluey felt a lump in his throat as he cautiously made his way around the perimeter of the deck, carefully studying the shadows, in search of the stalker. It was only a short distance, but it took him several minutes. Eventually he convinced himself that either he was imagining things or the stalker had given up.

He was now back in the area where the crane had dropped its load. The lifting strops were still attached to the crane hook, and they were all lying on the deck. Bluey examined the strops, expecting to see that they were damaged or broken. The strops were still in good condition and had a clear identification tag that showed that they had been inspected and tested just 10 days before. The eyes of the lifting strops were also still attached to the hook. It was clear to Bluey that the crate had not fallen because it had fallen away from the crane's lifting hook. The most likely cause, therefore, was that the crane brake had failed, or, alternatively, that there had been an operator error. Bluey had spoken to Moray, the production supervisor, in the canteen about the circumstances surrounding the crane failure incident. Moray had recalled that the crane driver's name was Jim, and that he had been in the canteen at the time of the incident. If the cause of the crane incident was operator error, then it certainly had not been caused by the regular driver. That suggested to Bluey that someone else had been at the controls of the crane when the crate was dropped. If that was the case, then either he or she was not a competent crane driver, or it had been intentional. On the other hand, being charitable, the crane brakes could have failed and the clandestine crane driver just hadn't wanted to be found doing a job that he or she was not trained for.

Bluey took one last look around the deck before starting to climb the hooped cat ladder up to the crane driver's cab. Rain was still lashing down and halfway up the ladder he paused to get his breath. As he leaned back on the safety hoops, he looked down at the deck and thought he saw a shadow move. Was it his eyes, or was it the stalker again? He was getting paranoid! Feel-

Duroc

ing vulnerable on the cat ladder, he pressed on to the top and lifted the hinged cover that allowed the only access into the crane's cab. In the half light from the deck floodlights, he looked around the small congested space for a light switch. After two failed attempts the cab lights came on. Bluey sat heavily in the driver's seat and studied the controls. The main controls consisted of joystick-type levers located on the arms of the seat, allowing the driver to slew the cab, raise the jib or raise or lower the load. It reminded Bluey of when he had hired a mini excavator to dig some foundations in the garden. It looked simple, as if anyone could make the functions work, but crane driving was an art form and needed considerable skill. His efforts with the excavator had nearly ended up with the jib and bucket going through the patio window! Debbie had said, "Maybe you should have got a man to do it!" That had really cut to the quick.

Suddenly there was a noise behind him. He looked over the back of the seat. The hinged cover in the floor at the top of the cat ladder was slowly starting to lift. Bluey couldn't see who it was because the cover hinged towards him and blocked his view. But he knew that it was the stalker. He grabbed a nearby large spanner and raised it above his head. A bright yellow hard hat appeared behind the open cover. Bluey was ready to strike the figure starting to emerge from the cat ladder.

"Oh—it's you!" The face of Moray Stewart was grinning over the edge of the hinged ladder cover. Moray swung himself into the cab as the cover dropped back to the floor. "I saw the cab light and thought I should see what was going on. Were you planning to welcome me?" he said, gesturing at the spanner in Bluey's raised hand.

Bluey was embarrassed and slowly put the spanner down before apologising and explaining what he was doing. His heart was racing but he was able to ask Moray if anyone other than Jim was authorised to drive the crane. Moray confirmed that there were only two qualified crane drivers, but said that at the moment the other driver was on days off, back on the mainland, so Jim had been the only driver on GG at the time of the incident. A second driver had just arrived on the chopper. It was very odd. Why would someone else want to tamper with the crane? Clearly some unqualified person had been at the crane controls that day. However, whoever it was, he or she was able to operate the crane and no one else had realised that it wasn't Jim driving.

Bluey told Moray that he wanted to inspect the hoist brakes. Moray pointed to a hatch in the back wall behind the seat. "It's through there, but be careful. Although the crane is fully isolated, once you go through the hatch you're in amongst the mechanism and the safety guard is the hatch." Moray checked the main electrical isolators on the cab wall. They were all off. He removed the interlock key from the main isolator and used it to unlock the hatch. "Just let me know when you're done," he said, and with a cheerful wave he lifted the hatch in the floor and climbed down the ladder. Bluey watched him descend the cat ladder, scanning what he could see of the main deck. It was starting to get late and there was no one else about. Apart from the shift production team, everyone else would be in the cinema or their rooms by now.

Bluey turned his attention to the unlocked hatch. It was quite small, and he had to get on all fours to crawl through to the mechanism compartment. It consisted of a tiny space filled with gearboxes and steel ropes. The ropes wound onto a large grooved drum which was driven by an electric motor. It was a brake motor which had a large disc brake at the free end of the motor. The brake shoes were firmly clamped onto the disc, indicating that the rope could not move. When the driver called for the crane rope to lower, the brake would be released and, simultaneously, the motor would start to turn. He checked the

Duroc

brake and found that it was firmly gripping the disc. There was no indication that the brake was slipping or malfunctioning. He pressed the test button on the brake's electric solenoid and the brake pads snapped open. When he released the test button the brake jaws slammed shut. There was nothing wrong with the brake.

"This failure was intentional!" he grimly said to himself. "Why would anyone want to intentionally cause a crate to drop from the crane?"

Bluey could only see two choices: either the crane operator had wanted to damage or destroy the contents of the crate, or he'd wanted to injure or kill Gus, the unlucky victim of the incident. This was not just an industrial incident—it could be attempted murder!

He turned towards the hatch to go back into the cab. He was on his knees again to crawl through the hatch. As he ducked his head to get through the opening, his hard hat fell off. As he stretched through the small opening to retrieve the hat, he saw a pair of safety boots and orange-coated leggings. But he never saw the swinging spanner. A searing pain burst through his head and everything went black as he slumped, unconscious, onto the floor.

A Rubik's cube tumbled out of his pocket, the puzzle still unfinished.

The assailant grinned to himself as he pushed the spanner-shaped weapon back into his trouser leg pocket. The Ashe inspector was asking too many questions, but he wouldn't be so inquisitive now. He picked up the Rubik's cube as a trophy. Moura would be pleased.

Chapter 9

Moura didn't seem exactly ecstatic. "What do you mean you've lost the consignment!" he yelled into the phone.

"The pig's stuck and we don't know where it is," came the reply.

"Well, you'd better bloody well find it!"

"They're planning to use a saturation diving vessel to search for it. The pig is carrying a tracer, so it shouldn't be too difficult."

"Well, you need to get someone onto the dive vessel to make sure that the consignment is recovered!"

"Our man on GG has just reported back. He took out an Ashe inspector, who was starting to ask too many questions."

"Oh, bloody brilliant! Interfering with the Ashe is as bad as interfering with the cops. They look after their own. Now we'll be overrun with the interfering so-and-so's." And he slammed the phone down.

*****

Moray Stewart was in the control room and it was getting towards the end of the shift. He was just completing his shift report and recording that the Ashe inspector had been investigating the crane failure incident. He paused for a moment—he hadn't heard back from the inspector. He called across the small control room to the panel operator at the console. The operator didn't know if the Ashe inspector had returned. Moray thought that he would go and check before signing off for the shift. He told the panel operator that he was going up to check the crane and then he would be going to his cabin in the accommodation module.

As Moray walked across the main deck towards the crane cat ladder, he saw that the crane cab lights were still on. Obviously Bluey was still working. He was about to turn to go to his cabin, when a sixth sense told him just to check the crane cab to be sure. He climbed up the cat ladder and pushed the floor flap open at the top.

He immediately saw a figure slumped across the floor, halfway out of the maintenance hatch at the back of the cab. The figure was not moving. He could see that it was Bluey, the Ashe inspector. Moray checked for a pulse. He was still alive. Moray barked into his radio, calling for the emergency response team. The production module tannoy immediately broadcast the need for the ERT team to go to the crane cab. In less than a minute the cat ladder was crawling with activity. The cab was starting to get congested. Three members of the team began to rig up ropes, to be able to stretcher the patient down from the awkward height of the crane. The others were administering first aid to the casualty. It looked as though he had been struck on the head. Moray suggested that he had been hit as he'd come out of the maintenance hatch. He'd probably never even seen his assailant.

The ERT team skilfully strapped Bluey's prone body onto the orange stretcher basket and carefully lowered him vertically down the crane cab cat ladder. As soon as he was at the main deck level, with three ERT men at each side of the basket, he was whisked away across the bridge and into the medical room.

The last 24 hours had been crazy for the rig paramedic. First it had been Gus, then the patients from the helicopter crash, and now Bluey. What was going on? It was like being in a war zone! The paramedic checked Bluey's vital signs. He was still alive, but obviously had a serious head injury, and he was very groggy. With the help of one of the ERT team, the paramedic wearily cleaned up the head injury and then bound Bluey's head with an elastic bandage. Moray Stewart came into the medical room and told the paramedic that Bluey was to be medevac'd to the Aberdeen Royal Infirmary on the first chopper in the morning. Having heard the medic's report, Moray told him to go and get his head down and Moray would arrange for one of the ERT Team to keep an eye on the casualties. The paramedic would be needed on the flight tomorrow to keep an eye on Bluey.

*****

It was 10 o'clock in the morning. Bluey had been sedated overnight, but he was now starting to recover some of his wits. He had had an unappetising breakfast of porridge and coffee. The porridge got left, but the coffee was good. Soon he was on his way to the helideck, being helped along by the paramedic. With the throbbing din of an S-92 dropping onto the helipad his head again felt as if it had burst open. As he climbed up to the red and white chopper, he caught sight of his bandaged head, looking like "Mr Bump," reflected in the chopper's window. It was hard work pulling himself inside, but his chaperone helped him up in a rather undignified way. As Bluey was strapped into his seat, various other rednecks were boarding. He recognised Stylo with a couple of others—obviously the "Drifters" had finished and were heading back home. The chopper was full, clearly the recent MedEvacs had delayed some people getting home for their scheduled rest days. Bluey closed his eyes for a moment and his head filled with images of hanging upside down in the helicopter with water just inches from his face. He quickly opened his eyes again. He didn't want to re-live yesterday's events. The guy in front of him had turned

Duroc

around and was asking how he was. What a stupid question. How did he think he was! Bluey whispered, "Oh, just dandy," with all the sarcasm he could muster. The guy in front ignored the inference and kept chatting as the rotor engines revved up for take-off. Bluey felt bad—the guy was obviously just trying to distract him from negative images of yesterday's crash. The Sikorsky roared into the air and soon the rig had disappeared from view, a mere speck in a maelstrom of grey sea.

The pulsing beat of the rotors had a hypnotic effect on Bluey and his attention waned until he was aroused by the voice of the paramedic, who was obviously concerned about delayed concussion. The paramedic just made small talk, asking about Bluey's wife and family and whether the boys were interested in football. They talked about how Stenhousemuir were struggling in the league, but conversation was difficult when competing with two General Electric jet engines. Voices were raised, to be audible above the din, but Bluey knew he had to stay awake and respond. The conversation moved to the work that he did. Yes, he worked for Ashe and this was his first visit to Gannet Gamma. It had not been an experience he wished to repeat! Yes, he'd been on the rig to investigate the crane failure. Would he be coming back? No. If more work was needed, he would send a colleague. Who would be coming in his place? In an unguarded moment, he let slip that his colleague was called Caitlin Barland and she would probably complete the crane failure investigation.

The guy in the seat in front of him smiled to himself, and scribbled the name "Caitlin Barland" on the back of his hand. Moura would be pleased. Maclean settled back in his seat and idly twirled the Rubik's cube that he had come across just yesterday.

Chapter 10

Caitlin was frustrated that she didn't seem to be getting anywhere with the bellows incident investigation at Duroc Petrochemicals. Sure, she understood the cause of the steam release and she understood how it had happened—Carl Dunne had either forgotten or just omitted to put all the backing rings back. But why? Was it just carelessness or was he lying? Perhaps the bigger question was who had told Carl to check the bellows, and, more importantly, why? At the back of her mind there was the niggling question about feedstock. Clearly the plant had been about to run out of feedstock. That was an operational problem. But how could inspecting the bellows magically create more feedstock? She wished that she could discuss it with Bluey, but he was enjoying himself out in the North Sea!

She picked up the phone and rang Iain at Duroc.

"Hi, Iain," she said. "Could I come over and look at the plant's list of inspection routines?"

Iain agreed, and 30 minutes later, after another hair-raising ride on the Triumph, she was at Duroc Petrochemicals browsing through the maintenance records. It was quickly very clear that there had been no routine requirement for an inspection of the compressor bellows. However, as she continued to scroll idly through the computer files, she came across a folder labelled "USP 1&2." The undersea pipelines were the supply routes for feedstock to the plant. They came ashore from the

Duroc

Gannet Gamma rig. She opened the first file; it contained all the details of the pipeline construction specifications. She scanned several other files until she came to a file entitled "Pigging." She clicked on the file and saw that it contained details of pigging programmes, with details of each time a pig was used. She called over to Iain, "Hey, what's this all about?"

Iain moved to look over her shoulder at the display screen and saw what it was. "It's just the pigging records," he said, adding, "We don't carry out pigging runs on the undersea pipelines, as they are GG's responsibility. But when the pigs calibrate the pipeline, we get sent copies of the results for our files."

Iain explained that there were two types of pigs used in the pipeline. The simpler and more common pig runs were used purely to separate the products, when there was a change of product specification. The other form of pig run used a sophisticated pig that could use ultrasonics to measure or calibrate the thickness of the pipeline walls. It was important to check for corrosion to ensure the safety of the pipelines and to prevent leakage.

"How often do they pig each pipe?" Caitlin asked.

"Well, the product separation pigs are run quite often, but the larger calibration pigs are only run about once every few years, unless there is a problem."

Caitlin clicked on the computer file marked "Pigging runs—calibration results." There were dozens of entries. Iain was surprised at the number of entries but explained that each file would contain very extensive continuous monitoring data, which needed expert interpretation. Caitlin clicked on the file labelled "14th July." It was empty. There was nothing there. She sampled about 10 other files—they were all empty!

Iain was dumbstruck. For a moment he couldn't speak. Then he felt the need to defend himself. "I don't look at the pigging results unless a problem is identified."

"Who identifies a problem?"

"That would be the pigging contractor."

"Who's that?"

"Well, GG use an outfit called Scottish Pipeline Services. We only see them when they come here to collect the pigs from the pig traps."

Something was going on. It was immediately obvious to Caitlin that for some reason there were far more maintenance pigging runs than was normal, but it was not clear that there were any real concerns about the thickness of the pipeline walls. She asked Iain for the contact details for Scottish Pipeline Services Ltd and then headed back to the office.

Once she was back at the Ashe offices, Caitlin settled at her desk, picked up the phone and rang Scottish Pipeline Services. A secretary answered the phone and told her that the crew who usually handled the USP pipeline pigging from Gannet Gamma were out at the rig on a job at the moment. There was a pause whilst she checked her computer and then she said that she thought they should be flying back now and were due at Dyce Airport in about an hour's time. She gave Caitlin a contact number for the team leader. She said his name was Stylo and that she would tell him that Ms Barland from Ashe had called.

Caitlin then thought that she should update Bluey on the situation at Duroc Petrochemicals. When she dialled his mobile number she didn't really expect an answer, as she thought he would be out on the rig, and that was a de-match area where naked flames and electronic equipment were forbidden. A female voice answered. "Who's that?" Caitlin asked.

"It's Debbie Scrimshaw. This is Bluey's phone."

"It's Caitlin. Could I have a word with Bluey, please?"

"Caitlin, I'm afraid Bluey isn't too good. He was attacked on the rig last night and he is on his way to the Royal Infirmary at Aberdeen. He's got a head injury, but I'll know more soon. I'm just about to drive up to Aberdeen." Caitlin could hear anxiety in Debbie's voice. She passed on her best wishes to Bluey and dropped the call. She called the Ashe boss and learned that he'd also been unaware. He warned Caitlin to be ready to go out to Gannet Gamma, if required. She said that she was booked on the next Helicopter Underwater Escape Training course, which started the day after tomorrow. She would be riding up to Aberdeen that night.

Caitlin worked on some paperwork for half an hour before she thought she would try and contact Stylo. She called the mobile number that she'd been given by the receptionist at Scottish Pipeline Services. When Stylo answered, she introduced herself. He seemed to be expecting the call and knew who she was. She mentioned that she might be needing to go out to the GG rig to carry out some investigation. Stylo was not very chatty, but he wanted to know why she was going.

"I have to finish the investigation into the crane failure incident, but I gather there has been another incident whilst pigging the undersea pipeline."

"Don't know anything about either of them," Stylo said.

"But didn't you launch a pig yesterday from the GG?"

"Well yes, but…"

"It didn't arrive."

"Oh… I didn't know that."

"Why are the records of the last pigging runs blank?" Caitlin asked.

"What?" Stylo seemed genuinely puzzled.

"The records at Duroc Petrochemicals—most of them are blank," Caitlin continued.

Stylo went silent for a moment and then he changed the subject. "You know that you have to have HUET training to fly out to the rig."

"Yep, I'm doing my training up in Aberdeen tomorrow." The line went dead.

Moura threw the phone receiver back into its stand and prowled around the room. Things were going wrong. First the chopper crash—but Maclean had put the Ashe inspector out of circulation for now. Stylo had just rung to say that another Ashe investigator had been asking questions, not just about the crane incident but also about pig runs. *They are getting too close for comfort.* Stylo had said that the replacement for the absent inspector was a young girl by the name of Caitlin Barland. Stylo had found out that she didn't yet have the necessary training to go out to the GG rig. Moura needed to get the "frighteners" put on her to get her to back off.

*****

It was Thursday and Caitlin had risen early to get her breakfast in the Rob Roy pub next to the budget hotel where she had spent the night. After a hearty breakfast that only young people have the appetite for, she rode the couple of miles up the road to the training centre on the Triumph Tiger in record time. Fortunately, this was not confirmed by the police! She needed to complete the HUET training course to be able to fly out to the North Sea rigs. The training centre was located on an out-of-town trading estate.

She parked in front of a modern brick-built office block that was integrated into a large industrial unit and had the words "Provident Offshore Training Ltd" emblazoned across the cladding of the main building. In Reception she found three other candidates for the training. She was the only female. The receptionist ushered them through to a small conference room where they were offered coffee and a brief introduction to the trainers and the plan for the day. The morning was taken up with tedious classroom emergency safety training, which in Caitlin's opinion was composed of statements of the blindingly obvious. The afternoon was to be spent on practical training in the pool, which was located in the larger building behind the offices.

Lunch was composed of a meagre selection of semi-dried up nibbles, washed down with a can of warm cola. There was a further short briefing after lunch, primarily to allow lunch to digest before the practical work began. Caitlin was shown the way to the ladies' changing room. She had been told to bring her swimming costume with her. She undressed and slipped into her blue and black one-piece speedo costume, stopping for a moment to glance in the mirror. She looked OK. In the locker there was a newly laundered orange jumpsuit and a yellow hard hat. She donned the jumpsuit over her costume, placed a scrunchy over her wrist and deftly flipped the scrunchy over a ponytail of golden locks before putting on the hard hat. The head band was too big if she was going to be able to see. She took the hat off, adjusted the nylon head band and chin strap, checked in the mirror again and decided that she was ready for public viewing—or she would be, once she had remembered to put her trainers on.

The four trainees assembled in the large building behind the offices. The three male candidates were clearly having difficultly pretending that they weren't ogling Caitlin. The group were assembled on the side of a specialised swimming pool. There were two black-clad scuba divers already in the water. Above them was a gantry crane with a large orange box-shaped structure suspended from the crane. The structure was obviously intended to represent part of the fuselage of a helicopter. Around the outside of the fuselage was a large circular beam with four small wheels at the top immediately below the crane hook. Caitlin surmised this was to allow the fuselage to rotate and simulate a capsize. The head trainer explained what was going to happen. Once they were all given their rebreathing devices, which would extend their breathing times underwater, they were ready to board the simulator. The scuba divers were there to assist them if anything went wrong with the escape.

There was a loud whirring sound as the overhead crane travelled above the pool, bringing the open end of the simulator to the pool side. The three oglers showed that they were capable of chivalry and indicated to Caitlin that she board first. She scrambled into the confined fuselage and took her seat at the front, looking out of the windscreen area, although there was no glass in the windows. The other three trainees took the remaining seats, one across the aisle from her and the other two directly behind. They all fastened their seat belts. Caitlin's heart raced; she was going to enjoy this. The crane trundled the fuselage back across the pool. Once in position the crane hoist operated and the fuselage was raised to about three metres above the surface of the water.

A voice came over the tannoy: "Everybody ready?" The two scuba divers gave the thumbs up sign, and, in sequence, each of the trainees indicated that they were ready. A klaxon sounded. The hoist started to drop the simulator into the water. After no more than three seconds it hit the water. Cold water started to flood into the fuselage. Caitlin felt her feet get wet. Then the fuselage started to rotate and capsize. Water was flooding in everywhere. In less than 13 seconds from the time the klaxon sounded the fuselage was fully submerged and upside down. Caitlin felt disorientated but remembered the morning's classroom training. *Stay calm. Use the breather. Release your seatbelt.* She felt for the seat belt buckle release and pressed. Nothing happened. Her full weight was on the belt, keeping the belt release from working. She squirmed around to get the belt to release. One of the other orange-suited trainees shot past her

Duroc

and in a flurry of bubbles he was out through the emergency door. She glanced behind. One of the two behind her was also struggling to release his belt. She couldn't see the third. She focussed her mind. All of a sudden, she got her belt buckle free and she sank downwards out of her seat. She was free! But then she felt a wrench in her right ankle. It was trapped. She couldn't free her foot! She pulled and jerked her ankle, but it wouldn't move. Luckily the water in the pool was crystal clear and she could see a strap around her ankle. She reached up to her ankle and pulled, but the strap wouldn't come free. It looked like the handle of a bag from the seat behind. This wasn't so much fun now. She looked around and saw that all the others had gone. She was starting to panic. How long would her air last? She had lost track of how long she had been underwater. She wasn't thinking clearly and didn't know what to do. Was this the cognitive paralysis they had talked about that morning in the classroom? Had someone done this on purpose? She thought she saw an evil man in black coming threateningly towards her. Wait, was he brandishing a knife? She wanted to scream, but under water no one hears you! Then she blacked out.

The man in the black wet-suit slashed through the webbing handle of the bag and gently pulled the girl's body out of the upturned seat. In two seconds they were out of the simulator and the other diver was there to help. Two of the three other trainees stared in horror, but one did not. He just smirked. Suddenly nearly everyone there was engaged in frantic activity. Caitlin was pulled to the side of the pool and the divers lifted her onto the cold tiled poolside. The lead trainer turned her on her front and water tumbled from her mouth. Her golden ponytail had lost all its appeal. The trainer checked that her mouth was clear, turned her over and listened for breathing. There was nothing. He pulled a mouthpiece from his chest pocket and gave her five rescue breaths. He leaned back and watched as her shapely chest started to rise and fall on its own. She was breathing again. Her eyes opened. The trainer helped her into a sitting position. She was freezing cold. Other hands were bringing blankets and a warm cup of tea. Caitlin grabbed the tea and mumbled apologies to her rescuers. The lead trainer asked her what had happened. She stuttered about getting her foot caught in some sort of strap. One of the scuba divers confirmed that fact.

After about 15 minutes Caitlin had regained her composure and was able to stand. The other trainees had already gone to get changed. She realized that if she was to get her certificate, she needed to get out of the simulator unaided. She told the lead trainer that she was ready to go again. He took some persuading, but she knew she needed to get out by herself.

The fuselage was raised out of the water. This time one of the divers would sit beside her in the fuselage. The whole process started again. The klaxon sounded, the simulator dropped and rotated, and, after just 30 seconds, a golden-haired trainee bobbed out of the simulator.

"She's a plucky one, that one," muttered the second diver.

The lead trainer helped Caitlin out of the pool, slapped her on the back by way of congratulations and told her to go and get showered and changed.

As she entered the changing room, she caught sight of a dishevelled apparition in the mirror. Was that her? No time to think. She stripped off the wet clothes and plunged into the steaming shower. The tingling warmth all over her naked body was bliss. The traumatic events of the afternoon were being washed away. After what seemed like an age, she turned off the shower, wrapped herself in a large white fluffy towel and stepped out into a distinctly steamy changing room. She went straight to the wall-mounted hair drier to dry her bedraggled locks. When done, she turned to the mirror to check on her

Duroc

workmanship and suddenly let out an audible gasp. The steam had condensed on the mirror and there, finger-written on the mirror, it said:

You were lucky this time. Stay away from the GG.

Chapter 11

The rain whipped down like needles in the merciless force 9 gale. Water cascaded off the chunky bows of the dive support vessel like lava from a volcano, as she ploughed her way up and down the gigantic heaving waves. Camera flashes of light illuminated the tortured scene, as lightning bounced around the horizon. The MS *Merganser* fought her way steadily towards the target—the Gannet Gamma. She was a 2600-tonne dwt (deadweight tonnage) specialist dive support vessel, built in Korea, with an overall length of 75 metres and a beam of 22 metres. Her powerful twin Caterpillar engines could push her along on a dead calm sea at 14 knots, but she wasn't managing that tonight. She had left Peterhead on the ebbing tide at twilight that afternoon. Her contract was to find a missing pipeline pig for Duroc Offshore. They should be at the GG by first light.

The departure from Peterhead had been so sudden that a few members of the crew and work teams were not aboard. Sometime in the next 24 hours they would be taking a chopper ride out to join the ship, assuming that the weather calmed down.

As the ship approached the Gannet sector of the North Sea, the wind and rain eased and the helmsman could pick out the lights of the Gannet Gamma rig on the horizon. They made radio contact with the rig and established that the pig was somewhere in the USP1 pipeline at a distance of somewhere between

Duroc

50 and 70 miles from the rig, assuming that it was travelling at the calculated speed before it got stuck. If the engineers were wrong and the pig seals were worn, or passing, then it could be much closer to the rig. The snag with navigating along an undersea pipeline was that you couldn't see it. So, the first problem was to find the pipe. The starting point was easy. Both undersea pipelines started from the rig's central production module. GPS indicated the route of the pipeline, and although that was accurate at the surface, there was many a slip between surface and pipe! And once the *Merganser* had found the pipeline, there was then the additional challenge of finding the pig.

The advantage of a high-tech sophisticated dive vessel was that finding undersea pipelines was their bread and butter. They planned to use a lightwork class of remotely operated underwater vehicle (an ROV) equipped with a special magnetometer to precisely locate the pipe. Once located, the manipulator arms would hold a Geiger counter to try and detect the radio activity being emitted by the pig. "Just like falling off a log, really," summed up the first mate, who sarcastically claimed that they had the simple task of finding the pig (which they couldn't see) in a pipeline (which they also couldn't see) located in several thousand square miles of North Sea and at depths of 90 metres! What could possibly go wrong?

The MS *Merganser* wasted no time in getting started. The GPS co-ordinates of each section of the pipeline were radioed from the rig to the dive ship and the deck officer started to navigate the route of the pipeline. It took just over five hours to reach the start point of the survey. The *Merganser*'s average speed was restricted to just over eight knots despite a calm sea, because of the need to accurately follow the GPS co-ordinates and because of a Sikorsky. At just after 2:00 p.m. the ship slowed on the receipt of a radio message of an incoming S-92. It was the *Merganser*'s missing crew members.

Simon W. Pain

The chopper circled the ship and then settled on the helipad mounted above the bridge. Six men tumbled out of the chopper and straight down the metal steps to the safety of the bridge. The S-92 didn't hang about. As soon as the passengers had disembarked, the pilot got the thumbs up, and after less than five minutes on the ship, the main engines thundered to a crescendo and the aircraft was back in the air, heading for its next pick-up before returning to Aberdeen.

The new arrivals reported to the master on the bridge. It was clear that the master knew four of the six well. They were regular crew members. He slapped them on the back, joshed with them for missing the departure from Peterhead and sent them down to their quarters. The two other arrivals were newcomers. Both were contractors; one was a welder and the other was from a company called Scottish Pipeline Services who knew something about pipeline pigs. The master introduced himself as Findlay Innes and welcomed the two onto the *Merganser*. He told the first mate to show the lads to their quarters, calling after them that there would be a briefing in the mess room at 5 o'clock.

The master noticed that when the welder stepped out of the bridge door, he bent down and picked something up. It seemed to be a Rubik's cube that must have dropped out of his pocket. He thought no more about it.

As the ship doggedly ploughed its way forward, there was activity on the main deck, a large low-lying area behind the foc'sle and helipad. It had what appeared to be a circular swimming pool in the deck, known as the "moonpool," through which the ROVs could be deployed. The inspection team were making use of the afternoon sunshine to carry out their checks on the Whimbrel ROV, named after the Scottish wading bird that was particularly adept at finding its prey when it was buried in the sand. The ROV followed in the footsteps of the mother ship and would be used to locate the pipeline and pig. They were testing the batteries and controls and, most importantly, the magnetometer that would detect the presence of the metal pipe as well as the Geiger counter that would be used to find the radiation from the pig.

At 5 o'clock, Findlay Innes summoned the key members of the crew and auxiliary teams into the mess room to brief them on the task at hand. The objective was to locate the missing pig. He said that they had been following the route of the USP1 pipeline and in the next couple of hours they would begin surveying in order to first locate the pipe and secondly to follow the pipe using the Geiger counter to identify the location of the stuck pig. What would happen once the pig was found was not yet clear, but they would await instructions from Duroc Offshore. The ROV team confirmed that the Whimbrel was ready for use, and so the decision was taken to start surveying as soon as the *Merganser* was 50 miles from the Gannet Gamma.

It was getting dark, but the sea was still unusually calm. It was ideal conditions for the ROV launch. The ship slowed to a standstill and held her position by the use of the multiple underwater azimuth thrusters. The deck area was suddenly flooded by lights as the Whimbrel was hoisted onto a davit and swung out over the moonpool. An umbilical cord connected the ROV via a cable drum to the operators located high up in the foc'sle, who were staring intently at their computer screens and completing the final checks before launch. The Whimbrel was steadily lowered into the water, the lifting strap was removed, and suddenly all that was visible were two beams of oddly greenish light. The beams stayed stationary for a few moments as the Whimbrel cleared the hull of the ship, and then it dived down, into the depths of the North Sea, where she could no longer be seen by the deck team.

The Whimbrel operators, safely located in the foc'sle control room watched their screens as the ROV danced its way down towards the seabed. Near the surface the water was very murky, but oddly it became clearer as she descended. The ship's sonar showed that the water depth was 90 metres, and so the ROV controllers slowed the Whimbrel's descent as it neared 80 metres. The ROV camera started to oscillate from side to side, the operators looking intently for signs of the pipeline. A shoal of gleaming sea lampreys chasséd their way across the screen. Suddenly, instead of blackness, the lights of the Whimbrel started to pick up topographical features. The camera swept backwards and forwards across the seabed. One of the operators said to no one in particular, "The pipe should be on top of the seabed." This was significant, because if the pipe were buried, then repair would be a much more difficult problem. The ROV then started to do a traverse, perpendicular to the direction of the pipe. This was the best way of finding the pipeline.

"What's that?" called one of the operators. Just at the edge of his screen there had been a shape. The operator nudged his joy stick and the ROV swung in an arc, coming back to check what had been seen. Out of the gloom they saw what appeared to be a small pipe sticking up. As the ROV came closer, they realised it was not a pipe. They saw that it was encrusted in barnacles and tapered in shape, and that another, similar pipe lay down beside it.

"Christ, it's a gun!" muttered the operator. As the Whimbrel approached the pipes it became clear this was not part of a pipeline but a sunken wreck. It appeared to be the partial remains of the rear gun emplacement of a World War I naval ship. Straight away the operators were googling "World War I wrecks in the North Sea". Mr Google came back with the suggestion that it could be HMS *Hawke*. The *Hawke* seemed to have been an ill-fated craft. Built in 1891, she was an Edgar class cruiser. In 1911 she had had a prang with the ocean liner RMS *Olympic*. The *Hawke* had suffered bow damage and the *Olympic*'s stern had been damaged. The operators mused that it sounded like bad driving with a rear-end shunt! On 15th October 1914, HMS *Hawke* was torpedoed in the North Sea off Aberdeen with the tragic loss of 524 of the crew of 594.

The operators were keen to try and identify the wreck. The Whimbrel hovered slowly around the hulk. The bows were not visible and so there was no sign of the identification number. Corrosion meant that the ship's superstructure had collapsed, and so no clear identifiers, such as funnel layout, were visible. The ROV supervisor logged the position of the wreck and instructed the team to leave the wreck and continue with the search for the pipeline. The search went on relentlessly for several hours, with the video monitors showing just desolate scenes from which the actors had long since fled. Eventually the batteries on the Whimbrel started to get low, and so she returned to the *Merganser* empty-handed.

The following morning, the ship re-adjusted its position and another sortie in the recharged Whimbrel was launched. This time they had more success. There, right in the middle of the control room video monitor, was the unmistakeable sign of a concrete-coated pipeline. And it was on the seabed, not buried. The ROV operator phoned the information through to the bridge and was given the order to switch on the Geiger counter and start following the pipeline. "Just make sure that you follow it east to west. We don't want to end up back at GG!" said Findlay Innes.

The Geiger counter was an addition to the usual equipment on the Whimbrel. It was firmly clamped in one of the manipulator arms of the ROV, but the actual radiation reading in millisieverts could not be transmitted via the ROV, so to detect the radiation the operators were merely listening for the increase in bleeping sounds from the meter. The source on the pig was not very strong, and so if the Whimbrel passed over too quickly, or the operators did not pay close attention, the location could be missed. It was very slow work. The *Merganser* was creeping forward to match the speed of the ROV. The ROV was limited by its battery life.

The work was so intense that, like an air traffic controller, an ROV operator could only stay focussed for about half an hour at a time before yielding to a colleague. After 70 hours they had followed the pipeline for just 10 miles. Suddenly, without warning, the Geiger counter sounds started to accelerate, going from monotonous occasional clicking to an almost continuous drone. The screens had everyone's attention. The operator let the Whimbrel continue to scan along the pipe. As it moved on, the Geiger counter reverted to just the occasional clicking. The operator steered the ROV in an arc and started to retrace its steps back along the pipeline. Lo and behold, the clicking started to increase again, until the operator held the Whimbrel stationary at the point where the noise was loudest.

They had found the missing pig!

The Whimbrel logged the co-ordinates and carefully recorded the details of the environment around the pig's location. The on-board cameras showed that the seabed in that area was relatively flat and there were no large outcrops of rock which could make repairs more complicated. The Whimbrel bobbed back up into the moonpool on the *Merganser*, its job complete.

Findlay Innes radioed the GG to report to Jason, the installation manager, that they had located the pig. The next question was, what did he want to do about it?

Chapter 12

Bluey was at home. It was three days since he had flown back from the GG. His head was feeling much better, but Debbie was fussing about him as if he was about to meet his Maker. The bandages had gone and he had had a CT scan at Aberdeen Royal Infirmary. There were no signs of serious damage, even though he still had headaches. He hadn't heard from Caitlin for the last couple of days, but he knew that she would be at the HUET training in Aberdeen, so he hadn't expected any calls, as the training would be quite straightforward. He was just idly watching the morning TV programmes when he heard the house telephone ring. Debbie answered it and appeared in the doorway, cradling the phone between her cheek and shoulder. Bluey thought she looked a picture.

"It's Caitlin," Debbie said. "Can she come over?"

Bluey spoke to Caitlin on the phone and agreed to her coming over later that afternoon, once he'd had a shave and made himself a bit more presentable.

Caitlin arrived at the house just after half past 3 on the lime green Tiger. Bluey watched her through the window as she removed her helmet and walked to the front door. She didn't seem to have her normal bounce. Debbie opened the door and ushered her into the lounge. As soon as Caitlin saw Bluey, her eyes welled up. She'd known that he hadn't been well, but he really looked as though he had been through the wars. He looked as though he had aged 10 years.

Bluey explained as much as he was able to remember about what had happened in the GG crane cab. He said that it was obvious that someone didn't want him sniffing around at Duroc Offshore.

"You're not the only one!" Caitlin said.

Bluey looked quizzical. "Why, what's happened?"

Caitlin explained what had happened during the helicopter underwater escape training. She was convinced that one of the other trainees had intentionally tried to stop her completing the training—or even worse. The tears that she'd been trying to hold back suddenly started to flow in intermittent sobs. Bluey stood up and gave her a fatherly hug.

"And that's not all," Caitlin said. She went on to explain that although she had completed a further escape exercise successfully, there had been the warning on the changing room mirror. "Bluey, I'm scared!" she exclaimed.

Bluey got her a stiff measure of Scotch from the wall cabinet and told her that it was their job to find out what was going on. He wondered how they'd known that Caitlin would be at the HUET training. When Caitlin had calmed down a bit, Bluey told her of some internet surfing that he had been doing the previous evening. He had been looking into the background of Duroc Offshore. When he had just typed in "Duroc," the first response that he got was: "*a reddish-brown pig.*"

"Doesn't that strike you as a bit of a co-incidence?" Bluey asked. "The company is named after a pig and it's a pig that has got stuck. Call me suspicious, but maybe everything is to do in some way with the pipeline pig."

"It's not just that," said Caitlin, "but the pig is stuck somewhere between Duroc Offshore's rig and Duroc Petrochemicals. Whatever is going on involves both the Duroc companies."

Duroc

"And whatever it is, there are some people who don't want either of us meddling in their affairs!" Bluey replied. "Why would they go to such lengths to try and stop our investigations?"

"This is about more than just run-of-the-mill industrial accidents," said Caitlin. "But what is significant about the pig?"

"I don't know, but I intend to find out. We need to be careful, though. This could be quite risky. We have both had uncomfortable experiences with helicopters in the last week, and we should take your mirror threat as a serious warning. Whatever we do, you shouldn't be working alone on this. If there is ever a need to go to Duroc installations, either onshore or offshore, you mustn't go alone."

Caitlin nodded. Now that she was with Bluey, she felt less scared. They started to brainstorm the possibilities as to why the stuck pig was of such significance, and whether it was likely that both Duroc Offshore and Duroc Petrochemicals were involved. There had now been four unexplained incidents in the last week, and three of those had occurred at Duroc installations: the boiler feed pump and bellows failures at the petrochemicals plant, and the crane failure and helicopter crash at GG. But there did not seem to be a common theme linking them, and none of them had involved pigs—until the pig had got stuck in the undersea pipeline. Bluey warned that they needed to be careful about who they discussed this matter with, until they knew more about what was really going on. Caitlin suggested that they refer to it as the "Enigma." That afternoon the Enigma project was born.

*****

The well-dressed businessman strode into the towering atrium of the National Gas & Energy Corporation's offices in London. The receptionist gave him a pleasant smile and a visitor's badge and told him to take the lift to the top floor, where he was expected. He took the glass-sided panoramic lift to his destination and was met by an attractive blonde secretary. She took his coat, asked if he would like a coffee, and then showed him into the board room to face an array of steely-eyed directors.

He introduced himself, although most of the directors knew him from his previous visits. The chairman was a no-nonsense character, and after welcoming the businessman he replaced his half-moon glasses, looked at the assembled directors and suggested that, as their visitor had arrived, they move directly to item 3 on the agenda.

"You are all aware of NG&E's plans to de-merge the UK gas transmission side of our business. We have been considering various options for that de-merger and, after much deliberation, we have eliminated all except one possible bidder."

The chairman bowed his head so that he could look directly at the newly arrived businessman over the top of his glasses. "You will be pleased to know that the Board has decided to recommend your offer to the shareholders," he said. The businessman smiled. "The deal obviously needs to be ratified by the shareholders at our AGM in November, but I do not anticipate any problems," continued the chairman. Looking around the room, he added, "I strongly remind all present that, as this decision is stock market-sensitive, there must be no discussion of the de-merger outside of this room. And now I suggest that we adjourn for a wee snifter, to celebrate the conclusion of a very satisfactory deal."

There were nods of approval and a few grunts around the table, before they collected up their papers and followed the chairman to form what looked for all the world like a geriatric conga dance, heading through a small door at the end of the

Duroc

room into what was referred to as the "juke joint." To the non-Americans present, it was just a private bar!

After several rounds of back slapping and more than a few of the obligatory "snifters," the meeting attendees returned in a semi-drunken state to the board room. The businessman bid his farewells and took the lift down to the ground floor. As he stopped at the reception desk, he smiled at the pretty receptionist, handed back his visitor's lanyard and was about to leave, when the receptionist politely reminded him to sign out. She proffered a lined book and a pen. He took both and without a moment's hesitation signed out. The receptionist smiled again and, as he walked towards the door, she read the last name in the visitor's book. All it said was "MOURA."

Moura hailed a black cab and returned to his hotel. He was pleased that he would shortly be able to launder some of his ill-gotten gains by investing in the UK's underground gas distribution system. This meant that the gas system would need lots of pigging. It certainly would be a distribution system, and for more than just gas! He could link his North Sea distribution network to almost anywhere in Scotland, or even the UK. His next acquisition could be the international interconnectors to Belgium!

His mobile pinged—there was a text message saying to call Stylo. He waited until he was in the confines of the hotel room to do so. It was a day of good news. The message was that the pig had been found in the USP1 pipeline, about 60 miles from Gannet Gamma.

Moura made some other calls. The problem now was how to remove the pig and its consignment without anyone learning its secret. The first task was to get the pipeline back in use, so that Duroc Petrochemicals could start up again. He discussed this with the team and they concluded that they needed to construct a by-pass around the pipe. Stylo said that the rig installation manager, Jason, had already concluded that a by-pass pipe would be needed.

However, breaking into the pipeline 80 to 90 metres below the surface was no small task. Moura indicated that until the by-pass was operating around the pig, no one would be aware of their secret. The challenge would be recovering the pig without too many questions being asked. In particular, he didn't want the Ashe people sticking their noses in. Stylo told him that the inspector was out of the picture for now, and that the girl had been given a scare! He didn't think that they would be back in a hurry. Moura told Stylo that he had some other news: the planned purchase of the national gas distribution network from NG&E. Stylo didn't seem impressed until Moura mentioned the need for pigging.

"But that's a consumer gas network," said Stylo. "The need for pigging is only occasional maintenance and corrosion checks. It's the liquid lines that use frequent pigging to separate the different products or grades."

"Ah! I'd thought about that. This will be different from the undersea pipelines. On the consumer gas transmission pipelines, if we own them, we can pig them as much as we like. And, what's more, they are really big pipes, so the pigs and consignments will be much bigger!" He sounded fanatical.

Chapter 13

Three days after the meeting at his house, Bluey was back at work in the Falkirk office. The other members of the office welcomed him back as if he were a long-lost brother, wanting to hear the stories of both the helicopter crash and the attack in the crane cab. After a certain amount of coffee drinking and not a lot of work, Bluey's boss sauntered in to tell him that the pig had been located. They discussed the consequences. Bluey wondered why the pig had got stuck and they mulled over how they could find out the cause, and whether there was any option to by-passing the pig. The more obvious choice was to try and move the pig.

"The problem is that we don't know what caused the pig to get stuck," said the boss.

"There are two possibilities," Bluey replied. "Either the pig is jammed on some physical obstruction, or else the pig cups are damaged and so there is not enough oomph to move the pig."

"We really ought to know which it is before committing to the risky and expensive job of a by-pass."

"It's not just the cost of the by-pass," Bluey added. "If there is a need to retrieve the pig, that is going to involve cutting and removing a section of the pipe. And that will be expensive."

"It would be cheaper to leave the pig down there."

"It would be cheaper, but it would cause problems in the future. Putting in the by-pass pipe would increase the pressure drop in the pipe, but also, more importantly, they wouldn't be able to pig the line ever again—pigs don't go around sharp corners very well! I think that for operational reasons Duroc will want to completely remove the pig, and then re-instate the pipe and remove the by-pass."

"So how can we find out why the pig got stuck?" asked the boss.

"There's only one way that I know of, and that's to X-ray the pipe."

"Can you X-ray something that has a radioactive source in it? Surely that would wipe out the X-ray image."

"Yeah, that could be a problem, but I can't think of any other way."

"OK, get in touch with Duroc Offshore and tell them that before they do anything else, we require them to radiograph the pipe to try and see why the pig was stuck. If the pig cups are worn, we may be able to chase it out with another pig."

"I'll get in touch with Jason Suinos, the IM at Gannet Gamma, today, and tell him," concluded Bluey.

Bluey immediately phoned Duroc Offshore and was put through to the installation manager. After Jason enquired about how he was, Bluey went on to explain that Ashe needed to establish why the pig had got stuck. To discover that, Ashe were asking for an X-ray of the pig's location.

There was a pause on the line. Jason's voice sounded agitated as he argued that that would just delay the time when they could start installing the by-pass and subsequently get the gas flowing again. He pointed out that Duroc Petrochemicals were shut down until they could receive feedstock from GG and, anyway, another underwater activity would just increase the risk to personnel and be costly.

Duroc

Bluey was used to dealing with such arguments—nearly everyone played the "can't afford it" card. "I'm not asking you, Jason, I'm telling you what Ashe requires you to do!"

And that was the end of the conversation. Phase 1 of Project Enigma was underway.

It didn't take long for word to get around Gannet Gamma that the pipe was to be radiographed. However, they weren't the ones on the scene, and so radio messages were sent to the MS *Merganser* to see whether the ship had radiographers on board. The answer was "no." There were no radiation sources on the ship and so there was normally no need for radiographers. However, sources and an underwater radiographer could be on the first flight out in the morning. The pipe was quite large in diameter and so it would need a reasonably sized X-ray source to get a good image, and that meant a large and heavy protective flask to prevent radiation leaks in transit. The source, in its lead protective flask, would weigh as much as several passengers, and although the radiation emitted from the outside of the flask was minimal, as a safety precaution the chopper would only carry its crew, the flask and the radiographers.

*****

Moura was livid, and he was taking it out on Stylo. "You need to stop this X-ray crap!"

"Firstly, it's not an X-ray, although people refer to it as that. An X-ray device requires electricity. We are talking here about using a gamma-ray source. Secondly, I can't stop it. If Ashe want it, then if we can't give a good reason why not, it has to happen. Ashe have more powers than the cops—so what they say goes!"

"What do you mean, it has to happen? I can think of a really good reason why it shouldn't happen. If they take an image of the pig, we—or, more precisely, you, are done for. Find a way to stop it!"

"It may not be a problem," said Stylo. "Remember the reason why we found the pig."

"You said you put a tracer on it."

"Exactly. It was a radioactive tracer. When the radiographic image is developed, they will find that the development of the image is totally or partially obliterated by the tracer. The image will just appear to be white."

"This is all on you, Stylo. You'd better be right!" Moura yelled, and with that he slammed down the phone.

*****

The North Sea was rough and the MS *Merganser* was pitching like a cork. It was just getting light and there was a Sikorsky S-92 heading towards the helipad over the foc'sle. It was carrying two industrial radiographics experts from Industrial Radiography Ltd. As the chopper hovered over the pitching helipad, a group of seafarers were on the steps below the helipad, ready to assist with removing the heavy radioisotope flask that was about to be delivered. As the rolling helipad slowly oscillated towards the level position, the chopper pilot skilfully dropped his aircraft onto the pad. The wheels were latched and the main door slid open. The two radiographers leapt out as the helipad started to pitch downwards. Upon shouted instructions from the Hamish McClurg, the *Merganser's* second mate, the waiting seafarers moved with cautious haste to collect the heavy cargo. Two of them clambered inside the chopper, unlashed the cylindrical flask, and rolled it towards the door.

There was a small crowd around the chopper door now. One of the Industrial Radiography men anticipated a problem and turned back towards the chopper, shouting, "Be careful!" But the warning was unheeded, either because of the noise from the chopper's engines or the weather. As he approached the door for a second time, the flask was on the threshold. What happened next was unclear, but the ship pitched again, the flask fell out of the helicopter and neither the radiographer nor any of assembled helpers could keep hold of it. It crashed onto the deck of the helipad and struck one of the seamen on the foot. He collapsed to the floor with a howl of nautical vocabulary. The flask started to slowly roll downhill. Men rushed after it. Hamish realised how risky that was. "Leave it!" he shouted.

The valuable flask trundled its way across the sloping helipad, but just as it neared the edge, the ship's pitch changed, and the flask paused for a moment before starting to retrace its way back across the helipad. Seamen gaped in awe, until they realised that this was some horrific game of pinball, in which they were the pins. Men scrambled into the helicopter and down the helipad steps in panic. Anywhere to avoid the hunting flask. The flask gathered speed and nobody was watching as it shot off the metal deck of the helipad and disappeared from sight.

From underneath the helipad, Hamish looked up and saw the radioisotope flask suspended precariously in the safety catch netting around the helipad. He called to the radiographer, who had just disembarked, and pointed to the flask. Three of the seamen ran to get lanyards and safety lines, as the recovery operation would be quite hazardous. One slip and they would not only end up in the drink, but they would have bounced against the superstructure on the way down. The three men lashed themselves to the structure and moved gingerly towards the edge of the helipad.

The landing deck was still gyrating about like a juggler's spinning plate. One moment the men seemed to be climbing uphill towards the flask, then suddenly the deck inclination changed from uphill to downhill and all three were on their backs, sliding towards the netting. Luckily, the safety lines did their job and all three came to an undignified halt just before they reached the edge of the deck. They stared through the netting at the heaving sea below. The flask was still in the net. After a short discussion, they decided that just one man should go out onto the netting. The lightest of the three took another line and very carefully inched out onto the netting.

Just at that moment, someone must have told the helicopter pilot that it was safe for him to take off. The engines revved up in a crescendo, causing a back-wash of air that caught the three seamen on the edge of the heli-deck. The man on the netting was blown straight off the edge and was left dangling like a spider above the sea.

Hamish screamed into his radio, "Stop the chopper from taking off— and tell that pilot to shut-down his engines!" As the engines subsided, Hamish grabbed a spare rope and ran around under the helipad until he was looking out at the dangling seaman. He threw an end of the line out to him, hoping that he could catch it. The line missed and fell down into the sea.

The ship was dipping to starboard in the swell, making the suspended seaman drift further from the ship's structure. Hamish pulled the rope back up, coiling it as he went, and then he waited for the swell to tilt the ship to port and bring the dangling seaman closer to the structure. Just as the seaman was at his closest, Hamish threw the line again. This time the seaman reached out and caught it, setting his suspension line swinging like a pendulum. By this time other members of the crew had joined Hamish on the walkway. They were all calling to the seaman to hang on, and they all joined in pulling him in to the ship. As he staggered over the ship's rail, the assembled crowd slapped him on the back. Hamish declared that the retrieval of the flask would have to wait until the sea swell had calmed.

Duroc

The following day, in calmer weather, the radiographic flask with its hazardous isotope contents was safely retrieved and brought to the main deck.

The two radiographers joined other members of the crew in the mess room. The lead radiographer was no stranger to the MS *Merganser*, but his usual assistant had been unavailable for this trip on account of a road traffic accident the previous evening. The replacement was a last-minute recruit who was apparently very familiar with diving operations in the North Sea. They chatted amiably about the plans for the radiography of the section of pipe where they had located the pig. Jock, the lead radiographer, asked if his new colleague could see the dive control centre so that he could become familiar with the video monitoring arrangements for the work. The newly recruited radiographer's assistant had little to say—in fact none of the crew caught his name.

At the end of the meal, the new recruit idly twirled a Rubik's cube. He wasn't able to complete the puzzle.

*****

The *Merganser* was a saturation diving vessel. This meant that she was equipped to allow for continuous diving operations. The problem with repeated deep dives was the fact that the divers were at risk of getting decompression sickness, or "the bends," each time they surfaced. In order to avoid this, it was necessary for the divers to return to the surface very slowly, so that the gases absorbed into the blood stream could degas. The *Merganser* was equipped with a series of hyperbaric chambers which enabled the divers to go back and forth between the seabed and the ship without coming out of the pressurised atmosphere. It was an amazing system, but very cramped.

Simon W. Pain

The following morning, after the flask had been recovered from the helipad netting, the two radiographers arrived in the dive control room to meet with the dive supervisor. They discussed the job of radiographing the pipe. The dive supervisor was particularly interested in how long the job would take. The duration of the job mattered, because it was a question of whether the two men were to remain on the seabed in the diving bell until the radiography was completed, or return to the hyperbaric chambers on the ship for that time. The pipeline was quite large, and for safety reasons the radio-isotope source that had arrived in the flask was not large. This meant quite a long exposure time in order to get a good image of the pipe and, hopefully, of the stuck pig. The dive supervisor immediately declared that they would need to return to the ship whilst the radiographic image was processing. The dive would take place the following morning.

As there were no diving operations underway, the radiographers were able to move their equipment and diving gear into one of the two hyperbaric chambers quite casually. The chamber was cylindrical in shape, with a narrow bunk bed down either side. Entry from the outside was at one end, with a sealed circular hatch at the other end which led to a short tunnel into the diving bell. Beyond that was a second chamber to allow another team of divers to be sleeping whilst the first chamber was in use by the working divers. Once inside the pressurised hyperbaric system, the divers could stay in the special helium/oxygen atmosphere without the risk of getting the bends for many days. Beyond the second chamber was the hyperbaric lifeboat so that, in the event of an emergency, the divers would not need to depressurise before abandoning ship. Everything had been thought of.

Duroc

The dive supervisor had instructed the radiographers to ensure that they slept in the hyperbaric chamber as it could be slowly pressurised overnight in readiness for the morning's dive. They selected their meal menus and finally entered the chamber early in the evening. The heavy circular door clanged shut and the red indicator light glowed to indicate that the door was locked and that they were now effectively imprisoned. This feeling of being "detained at His Majesty's pleasure" was further reinforced by the fact that the two men were being continuously watched on CCTV from the dive control room. The newcomer clearly didn't like the feeling of claustrophobia and he started to go cold and clammy. He lay on the bed whilst Jock, the lead radiographer, took out a laptop, plugged the cable into the wall socket and started to surf the internet in search of a film to watch to while away the time.

The tannoy crackled with the voice of the dive supervisor. "You guys OK?" The senior radiographer turned to the camera and gave a "thumbs up" sign. There was little discussion in the chamber that evening, with one man glued to his laptop and the other tossing and turning on his bunk. A fairly basic meal arrived in the small airlock and was heartily received by one, but not by the other. Eventually, at 10:30 p.m., the overhead lights turned to red, the laptop was switched off and both men attempted to get some sleep under the ever-watchful eye of the CCTV.

*****

At 6 o'clock in the morning a buzzer sounded. It would have disturbed their slumber if either of them had been asleep, but, as it was, they were both wide awake, just waiting for the call to action. They called the control room to confirm they were awake, and had a light breakfast before checking over their diving gear. At about 6:45 a.m. they were given permission by the dive supervisor to transfer through to the diving bell. The term "bell" was a complete misnomer. The "bell" was actually a pressurised metal sphere surrounded by a cage structure for protection and stability. The *Merganser* was home to two diving bells; the crew had given them the nicknames of Liberty and Big Ben after other famous bells.

Liberty would be their taxi down to the pipeline. Jock and his mate—Jock had established he was known as "Bogie"—crawled through the short tunnel between the chamber and the bell, entering the Liberty from the side through a small circular door. She was already at pressure, with the air mixture, communications link, and power all being supplied through an umbilical cord attached to the top of the bell. Bogie took on the role of the "bellman." He would be the safety contact between Jock in the water and the dive supervisor. The space was distinctly "bijou," and although designed to take four divers, it was pretty congested with Jock, Bogie and their assorted pieces of equipment.

Jock pulled the circular access door closed and spun the locking wheel. A red light lit up above the door, confirming the door was locked and watertight. Jock got Bogie to check that they had everything that they were going to need for the radiography job. Then they checked that the internal pressure was OK and told the dive supervisor that they were "ready to go." There was a dull thump as Liberty was detached from the link tunnel, and the next moment she was dangling on the main hoist cable and starting to sink into the water through the moonpool. Bogie looked anxiously through one of the portholes in the upper half of the bell. Initially he saw lights from below decks on the *Merganser*, and then water washed over the porthole and they were on their way to the depths. Bogie glanced anxiously through one of the upper portholes at the shape of the *Merganser*'s hull, black against the lighter sea. He could see the line of bubbles from the azimuth thrusters that were slowly

Duroc

turning below the bow of the ship, automatically keeping the ship on its GPS station.

As the Liberty gently subsided on its way towards the sea floor, the two radiographers busied themselves donning their diving suits. Despite the cramped conditions, the continuous flow of air was keeping them comfortable. There was a monotonous report from the dive controller detailing their depth. Eventually, the message "Five metres to touchdown" came, and a few moments later the bell structure found the seabed and settled at a slight list to one side. Jock reported the landing to the control room and checked that the internal and external pressures matched. This time they would depart through a large circular hatch in the floor. Once the dive supervisor had given the OK, the hatch was unlocked and the two men carefully lifted it to one side. To the untrained eye, it would have been astonishing to see that when the hatch was lifted the water didn't suddenly rush into the bell! However, the pressures were completely in balance, keeping the water level at bay. Josh turned on the lights outside the bell and suddenly the black nothingness was transformed into an underwater monochrome wonderland of rocks, marine life, and a pipeline.

Jock slipped through the hatch into the icy cold water. He was breathing via a long breather pipe rather than cylinders. He looked up into Liberty and indicated to Bogie to pass down the Geiger counter; then he set off to check the exact location of the pig. The GPS locating device on the ship was working well, and he found the radioactive tracer on the pig no more than 20 metres away from the bell.

Jock marked up the outside of the pipe with a wax crayon and headed straight back to Liberty. The dive support crew had strapped the isotope flask onto the bell support structure during the night and so, after stowing the Geiger counter—and contrary to all the bellman rules—Bogie joined his mate outside the bell and started to release the webbing straps which held the flask to the Liberty's support legs. The buoyancy of the water made handling the heavy flask much easier, and they soon had it secured onto the pipeline at the location where Jock thought he had located the pig. Taking the radiographs under water involved vintage technology and so Jock secured the exposure film to the far side of the pipeline. There was to be no digital imaging on this job! Jock gave the diver's traditional "OK" sign to Bogie and indicated that he should return to Liberty. Once Bogie was in the bell, Jock slid the shutter open on the isotope flask to start the radiographic process. He immediately moved away from the flask and headed back to the bell to join his mate. He clambered inside the cramped space, removing the mask and breather tube as he went. Bogie was already on the intercom, informing the dive supervisor that the isotope and film were in position. They then replaced and locked the hatch in the floor and indicated to the control room that they were ready to ascend. The trip back to the *Merganser* went without incident, and they were soon climbing out of the diving bell and crawling through the tunnel back to their temporary home in the hyperbaric chamber. The whole trip had taken just over an hour.

The two radiographers were ready for a good meal, and after that they whiled away the time until they were ready to return to collect the exposed radiographic image. Jock completed the dive log whilst Bogie had his head in a book. At 4 p.m. it was time to return to the seabed and get the completed radiograph. As with the previous journey back to the ship, the descent to the seabed was straightforward and without incident. Jock went out to the flask first of all, to close the shutter on the flask in order to stop the gamma-ray emissions. Bogie watched the beam of light from Jock's helmet torch focussing on the flask. Jock turned and beckoned to Bogie to come and help lift the flask off the pipe.

Bogie shivered as he slipped through the hatch into the water and made his way across the seabed to help his colleague. They quickly recovered the flask and strapped it back onto one of the legs of the diving bell, before entering Liberty and preparing for the final ascent.

The job was done, and all they had to do was enjoy the short ride back up to the *Merganser*. They confirmed to the control room that the job was complete, that Liberty was watertight again, and that they were ready for the ascent. The dive supervisor confirmed that the weather had deteriorated and that there was now a significant swell on the sea. To add to that, one of the bow thrusters was giving problems and that meant that the *Merganser* was having difficulty staying on station. He was keen to get Liberty back on board as soon as possible. The radiographers confirmed that that was their intention also! The slight lateral movement of the ship meant that the main hoist rope was no longer vertical, but at a slight angle. As the hoist started to take the Liberty's weight, the bell lurched sideways, throwing Jock on top of Bogie. There was a sudden crash and Liberty fell over.

"Stop!!" screamed Jock.

The dive supervisor looked at the CCTV and saw the chaos inside the bell. "Stop the hoist!" he called, and the large winch suddenly stopped. "Lower the hoist again." But it made no difference to Liberty—it was completely on its side. "You OK?" asked the supervisor.

"Aye, I think so!" called Jock. "What happened?"

"Don't know. You'll need to go out and have a look."

They were unable to use the floor hatch, as that was now in a vertical position and opening it would just have blown the air out of the bell. They would have to use the main access door, which was now effectively on the bottom. Clearly Bogie was in no fit state to go out of the bell, and so Jock reconnected his air supply, checked his helmet light, and slipped back into the freezing water. He switched on his helmet camera so that the pictures could be transmitted back to the *Merganser*.

The images on the control room screens showed the diving bell was lying on its side. Jock's light was flickering across the base and support legs of the bell. It was immediately obvious that with the slight sideways pull from the off-station *Merganser*, the bell had been dragged sideways, just a few metres, but sufficient for the base to catch on a rock and to cause Liberty to topple over. Jock checked around the bell, but there was no sign of any damage. The isotope flask was still there. He headed back to the open doorway underneath the bell and clambered back inside to be met by a worried look from Bogie. They closed the circular door and luckily the red light came on again, signifying the door was locked and watertight.

Jock reported back to the dive supervisor that other than the bell being on its side, it did not seem to have sustained any damage.

"We'll need to reposition the *Merganser* once the swell dies down," said the supervisor. "Then we can pull you upright again. The weather's still bad up here, so you might be down there for a while."

Just what they needed! Another few hours in Davy Jones's Locker, with nothing to do but wait and worry.

Sitting in an upturned diving bell has nothing to recommend it. The radiographers hardly knew each other and had little in common. Jock tried to get Bogie talking, but he was not very forthcoming. One thoughtful person in the control room was quietly playing Vivaldi's "Four Seasons" over the bell's communications link. It didn't help. The time dragged very slowly. Eventually the imprisoned radiographers tried to get some sleep, but their minds were racing. After what seemed like months of waiting, suddenly Mr Vivaldi's band stopped in mid semi-quaver.

"Jock, Bogie, are you awake?" It was the dive supervisor.

"Aye," grunted Jock.

"Weather's better up here. The ship's back on station and the thruster is repaired. In a few minutes we're going to start winching again. You'll need to be in the bottom corner."

"Bloody brilliant," retorted Bogie with a scowl. "Which part of this sphere is the bottom corner?!"

Jock smiled. "Try there," he said, pointing to the left of the floor hatch.

After a few moments waiting, the dive supervisor's voice came over the intercom. "Hold on, we're starting to winch."

Nothing happened. The radiographers looked at each other, but neither spoke.

Then they started to feel some movement. There were creaking sounds from the underside of the Liberty's structure. The outside lights were still on. Jock looked out—the porthole which should have looked sideways was looking straight up, but the *Merganser* was too far away to see, and in any case it was probably dark by now. Liberty was still slowly righting itself. There was a crunch and the structure under the bell obviously came clear of the rock and Liberty was righting itself with alarming speed. Would it stop when it got upright or would the momentum make it fall over the other way? They didn't know, but they didn't have to wait long. No sooner was the bell upright, than it kept going like a rocking horse, with nothing to prevent it falling over the other way. The two men rushed to the opposite side of the bell, desperately trying to compensate for the overshoot because most of the weight was at the top of the bell. They hung onto each other as the centre of gravity of the bell slowly approached the point of no return, which would mean Liberty falling over again. They held their breaths, but it never got there. Before the bell toppled it started to rock back towards the stable central position. The radiographers lurched in unison back across the bell to stop yet another overshoot. The bell overshot slightly, rocked back again, and then settled firmly upright on its legs. Jock and Bogie fell in a heap on the floor, physically and mentally exhausted. No one spoke.

Finally, the dive supervisor broke the silence. "What just happened?"

"Never mind. Get us the **** out of here!"

Winching continued and Jock could see puffs of sand billowing in the bell's floodlights as it eventually left the seabed behind.

Suddenly there was an almighty metallic clang on the top of the bell. Liberty dropped and bounced several times, as if on the end of a spring. Jock, who had just been standing to clear some debris in order to sit down, lurched sideways and fell heavily against the main door. He slumped to the floor. Bogie jumped up and called out to him. Jock didn't speak. There was blood seeping from his head. Bogie looked up to see blood on the main door hand wheel where Jock had hit his head.

"Man down!" yelled Bogie into the intercom.

"Never mind that—you're off the hoist!" came the reply. "We've had to stop winching. The only thing connecting you to the *Merganser* is the umbilical."

Bogie wasn't very experienced with diving bells, but he knew enough to understand that the air pipe and some flimsy electrical cables were not intended to lift a steel diving bell and all its ballast.

Bogie stared out of the portholes and saw that the floodlights showed the seabed gradually receding. Liberty was starting to rise again. He turned his attention to Jock. He was still out cold but had a strong pulse, or was that Bogie's heart thumping in his chest? He tried to make Jock as comfortable as possible, cushioning his head with a rolled-up life jacket. He took out the very basic first aid kit and started to clean up Jock's injury, but it was more to keep himself occupied, rather than with any expectation of helping his colleague's recovery. As he finished, he became aware that the background sounds in the bell had changed. The steady hiss of the air supply was much quieter. He told this to the dive supervisor over the intercom.

"It'll be the weight of the bell," the dive supervisor replied. "The umbilical is taking all the weight and that could be crushing the air pipe." He turned to the team in the dive control room, and said, "We need to get them up—their air supply is restricted!"

The speed of winding the umbilical was increased. At the same time, as a precautionary measure, the dive supervisor ordered a dive team from the second hyperbaric chamber to prepare to launch Big Ben, the *Merganser*'s second diving bell. Just in case a rescue was required.

Bogie sat fretting in the debilitated bell. Jock was stable but not yet conscious. Suddenly there was a rushing sound of air escaping. Once again Bogie looked out of the porthole at the blackness, but this time fish were going upwards past the porthole. Liberty was falling! Bogie yelled into the intercom, "We're falling!" He suddenly realised that the umbilical must have snapped. Air was bleeding out of the bell through the broken umbilical, and that meant the pressure was dropping. Bogie knew that could mean a risk of "the bends." Without thinking, he grabbed a small emergency air cylinder and smashed the plastic grill over the air inlet. He ripped a piece of black rubber from his diving suit and jammed it into the air inlet hole to stem the leak of air out of the bell. Just as he thought his problems were solved, the power cables, which were the only thing left linking the bell to the *Merganser*, became stretched to such an extent that they broke. The interior and outside floodlights on the bell blacked out. The soothing tones of Vivaldi's "Four Seasons" went silent. Bogie and the comatose Jock were left incommunicado as the wayward bell plunged back towards the seabed. Luckily, it was not far, and for the second time in the last ten minutes, the bell ended up on its side on the seabed.

There was panic in the dive control room on the *Merganser*. All links with Liberty had now been lost and it had to be assumed that the bell had fallen back to the seabed. They had no way of knowing that Bogie had stemmed the leak of air from the bell. They had to assume that it was de-pressuring. The dive supervisor checked that the second diving bell was ready for launch. It was. Big Ben, the rescue bell, contained a crew of three, made up of two fully equipped divers and a bellman. Finding the defunct Liberty should not be a problem, as the *Merganser* was now holding its position, but whether there would be anyone alive in it was a different question. A torrent of communications streamed to and from Big Ben. The depth was being steadily called as the rescue bell continued its descent. The outside floodlights were on now, but the screens in the *Merganser* were only showing eerie green water with just the occasional sign of sea life floating past the portholes. The ROV had also been launched and was heading into the depths. It was less constrained by cumbersome air pipes and so it approached the seabed more quickly.

Bogie thought that his end was nigh. He wasn't sure what was happening, but in the absence of any other information, his brain was assuming the worst. He couldn't do anything more for Jock. It was just too dark. All he had was his small helmet head lamp. He was checking over his diving suit and trying to don the escape set, just in case he had to make a break for it, but as the pressure gradually dropped, the chances of safely

Duroc

opening the hatch diminished. Not only that, but his escape set wouldn't allow him time to get to the surface without getting "the bends." He was looking out of a porthole—at least he thought he was. All he could see was blackness. Maybe he was staring at the wall! Then he saw it. In the total darkness he got a glimpse of some lights high above. The orientation of the lights indicated that it was the ROV. They were coming to look for him! It seemed like an eternity before the lights approached the stricken bell.

In the control room, the ROV operator called out that he had Liberty in sight. He reported that the bell was on its side. The ROV danced its way around the hulk of the bell. There didn't seem to be any significant impact damage, but it was clear that all the service connections were severed. As the lights of the ROV fell on a porthole, the dive supervisor said, "Go in closer." The ROV operator brought a close-up of the porthole onto the screen. There was no one there.

Bogie saw the bright lights come to the porthole behind him. The light was dazzling after all the darkness. He groped his way across the bell, trying to avoid standing on the prone body of his colleague. Just as he got his face to the port hole, the ROV's lights turned away to search elsewhere.

"Try the other port holes," said the dive supervisor. The lights scanned across Liberty, which lay lazily on the seabed. There was no face at the second porthole either. As the third one came onto the screen, there was also nothing there.

"Wait, something's moving," said the ROV operator. And as he spoke, Bogie's face came into the circular frame. "That's the new bellman," confirmed one of the group clustered around the computer screen.

The dive supervisor told the rescue bell that someone was still alive in the damaged bell. At about the same time, Bogie noticed the floodlights of the other diving bell somewhere above him. Perhaps he would be rescued after all?

The ROV continued to hover over the damaged bell, trying to establish why the main hoist cable had come adrift. The main cable was nowhere to be seen, but the shackle that connected it to the top of the bell was missing, and there were no remains of a broken cable. It was starting to look as though the large D-shaped shackle which joined the cable to the bell had just come unscrewed. Once that had come adrift, all the weight would have been transferred to the umbilical.

Big Ben, the rescue bell, was reporting a sighting of the fallen bell. With a puff of sand, Big Ben settled onto the seabed less than 10 metres from its quarry. The lead diver was cleared by the dive supervisor to leave Big Ben to investigate. The floor-based hatch was opened and the lead diver slipped into the icy water and headed across to see Bogie. He shone his torchlight into the damaged bell and could make out the two figures of Bogie and Jock. The one was already in diving gear, and the second, although still in diving gear, was lying on what appeared to be the bottom of the bell, but because Liberty was on its side he was actually lying on the side wall.

The rescue diver indicated to Bogie through the porthole that he should check the pressure in the bell, and that if it was still OK he should ensure that Jock's head was not on the floor. He could then try and open the side door. Bogie gave the OK sign, showing that he understood, and in the light of his rescuer's torch shining through the porthole, he carefully lifted Jock's head and propped him up in a more comfortable sitting position.

There were banging sounds on Liberty's door and then the door burst open and the head of a rescue diver bobbed up. The diver came into the cramped bell to check over Jock. His vital signs were OK but he was still out cold. They would first get

Duroc

Jock out of the bell and on his way to Big Ben, and then Bogie could follow.

A second rescue diver was now at the hatch. Both men inside the bell positioned the comatose Jock over the main hatch and then the rescue diver slipped back into the water, indicating to Bogie to guide Jock through the main doorway. Once Jock was out and in the capable arms of the two rescue divers, Bogie donned his headset and without a hint of farewell rushed out of the stricken Liberty. As he swam past the hulk of Liberty, towards the safe-haven of Big Ben, he noticed in the lights of the ROV that there was no hoist cable and no umbilical connected to Liberty.

Inside Big Ben, it was like a sardine can crammed with the lifeless body of Jock and four others. Once Jock was safely installed in Big Ben, the two rescue divers went back out to reconnect the hoist wire to Liberty. This only took about half an hour, as Liberty's hoist cable was still intact, and it was confirmed that it had just become disconnected and had not broken. Once the two rescue divers had returned to Big Ben, the dive supervisor gave permission for the rescue bell to return to the *Merganser* and discharge the occupants into the two decompression chambers.

In the control room, the team had their eyes on the computer screens as the cameras on the ROV recorded their efforts to recover the Liberty. The bell slowly started to rise into the normal vertical position. The camera zoomed in as the bell steadied itself. Something was swishing about in one of the portholes. "Is that what I think it is?" muttered the dive supervisor. One of the onlookers casually commented that it looked like a Rubik's cube.

*****

The following morning, Jock was to be medevac'd to Aberdeen. Bogie took the same flight, together with the heavy isotope flask and the completed radiographic images of the pipeline. The failure of Liberty's hoist was declared as a dangerous incident and reported by email to Ashe. The regulator might want to investigate it further. Liberty was given a thorough overhaul and declared safe to use, provided that locking devices were placed on the hoist shackle.

None of the crew noticed that the Rubik's cube that had been seen in the porthole was no longer there.

Chapter 14

The early Sunday morning light shone with an orange glow on the world's largest equine sculptures. Caitlin stopped her early morning run to gaze again at the amazing shining Kelpies. She did that every time she jogged around Helix Park, which was the home of these two impressive, hundred-foot-tall horses' heads, which represented the role that heavy horses had played in Scotland's development. In Scottish folklore, kelpies were beautiful aquatic creatures that were alleged to take on the forms of both horses and humans. Although the sculptures looked stunning, they represented dangerous creatures that could lure people to their deaths by coming to the shore. They could take on the head of a horse, with the body of an eel. The sculptures took her breath away each time she saw them—or at least she thought they did, but perhaps she was just looking for an excuse to have a rest to recover from the run! There was only one other person looking at the Kelpies at that time in the morning and he looked as though he had been there for some time. The vagrant was sipping some clear liquid from an unlabelled bottle, and she guessed that it wasn't just water. She nodded a greeting and then guiltily turned away from the ragged figure and hastily jogged off towards the car park. The exercise always made her feel good first thing in the morning. She had done it nearly every day since she had been at university and the benefit showed in her lithe figure. She rode the Triumph back home through the streets of Falkirk where there were signs that the residents were starting to emerge from their slumbers and head to work.

After a quick shower and a typical student's meagre breakfast, she headed into the Ashe office. Bluey was already there. He had a coffee in one hand and his computer mouse in the other. He was studying the morning's emails. He had fully recovered from the attack in the crane cab on Gannet Gamma and was back to his usual energetic self.

Once Caitlin had got the essential morning pick-you-up cup of coffee, Bluey called her over to his computer screen.

"We've had an email from Scottish Pipeline Services. They've completed the radiograph on the Duroc pipeline. Do you want to have a look?"

Caitlin skated over to his desk on her five-wheeled swivel chair. "What's it show?"

Bluey opened the email attachment. There was just one image. It clearly showed the typical black and white photographic negative-style view—that was normal with a radiograph. They both gazed at the image on the screen. It was the first time that Caitlin had seen an industrial radiograph. The picture seemed to show a reasonably clear view of a piece of pipe with some sort of device inside it. Bluey pointed out the thick white lines that represented the walls of the pipe. There was a timestamp in the bottom right corner of the image, indicating that the exposure had occurred two days earlier.

Bluey explained to Caitlin what was in the image. "See, this is one of the cups of the pig," he said, pointing to a toilet-plunger shape on the image, "and there's another one at the other end. As this pig is intended just to travel in one direction, the cups both face in the same direction."

"What are these for?" asked Caitlin, pointing to some vertical white lines on the image between the two cups.

Duroc

"Those are side views of discs between the cups. I'm no expert in pigging, but the cups are used to push the pig through the pipe, and the discs help separate the products in front of and behind the pig."

"So, this pig would be used to separate two different products in the pipeline?"

"Yes, I think so. There are lots of different types of pigs; some are used to separate different products, but others are used for cleaning the inside of the pipe, or even for checking the cross-sectional shape of the pipe or its wall thickness." Bluey was studying the screen intently. "What's strange is that the pig seems to be in very good condition—in fact I would say it looks brand new, even though it must have travelled over 60 miles There is no sign of wear at all."

"So why did it become stuck? Shouldn't there be some sign of wear, or something jamming the cups?"

"Absolutely!" agreed Bluey. "If this pig is still in good condition, and there is no obstruction in the pipe, then why did it stop?"

"It would stop if the compressor on the GG rig stopped working," suggested Caitlin.

"Yes, but we know that the compressor, or at least the pressure, was still on in the pipeline. That's what caused the chopper to crash. If pumping into the pipeline had stopped, then the relief valve wouldn't have lifted and discharged up the flare. It was the sudden flaring that engulfed the helicopter and caused the crash."

"So, what you are saying is... we know there was plenty of pressure to propel the pig?"

"Yep,"

"So why did the pig stop, then?"

Bluey replied, "I can only think of two other possibilities. Either the cups on the pig were damaged or worn, or the pig hit something and got stuck. If it hit something, then there should be an obstacle showing on the radiograph."

"Look at the image. There's no sign of anything jamming the pig," Caitlin said.

"Yes, and the pig cups seem to be in contact with the pipe wall, so very little could pass by it," Bluey added.

Caitlin summarised, "So, what you're saying is—there was plenty of pressure, nothing much could by-pass the pig cups, and the pig wasn't jammed on anything! In other words, the pig should have carried on to the end of the pipe."

Bluey nodded. "There's something we are missing."

Bluey and Caitlin studied the image on the computer screen for several more minutes, until the phone rang. It was a ship-to-shore call. The caller introduced himself as Findlay Innes, the master of the MS *Merganser*, a saturation diving vessel that was under contract to Duroc Offshore. Bluey's ears pricked up. The reason for the call was to confirm that two days earlier there had been a diving incident. One of the *Merganser*'s diving bells had come adrift from its hoisting cable. There had been one minor injury but everything was alright now. Bluey begged to differ and indicated that Ashe representatives would need to visit the vessel. He said that he would call back when they had made suitable arrangements, then dropped the call.

"Guess what?" he called to Caitlin.

"What?"

"The enigma project has a new development. There's been a diving incident on a ship called the MS *Merganser*. It's under contract to none other than Duroc Offshore. I'll bet you anything you like that the incident happened whilst they were looking for the infamous pig!"

Caitlin grinned.

Duroc

"You make the arrangements for both of us to go out to the *Merganser*," Bluey said, "and I'm going to find someone who knows about pigging to speak to."

Mr Google told Bluey that there was research into pipeline pigging going on at Strathclyde University. The contact was a Professor Irving Grant. He was an amiable academic, whose only curse was the fact that he had been promoted to the enviable heights of professor some years before, only to find that the title "professor" made it possible for the disrespectful students to abbreviate his initials as "Prof IG," or "PIG," for short. He was now universally known as "Oink."

Bluey called Oink and introduced himself. He explained what had happened in the undersea pipeline and that they had asked for a radiographic image of the stuck pig. The professor asked to see a copy of the image. Bluey immediately emailed it and Oink called back within a few minutes. He agreed that there was something very unusual about the image. Two things immediately struck him. First of all, the radiography was remarkably good, given that it had been taken on the seabed. He thought that both the pig and the pipe looked almost brand new. A bigger concern was the pipe material. Oink asked what type of material it was and what its thickness and age would be. Bluey said he didn't know at that moment, but he would find out. Oink said that he had extensive experience of underwater pipelines and that usually pipelines on the seabed had to be weighted down in some way, so that in the event that they were emptied, they didn't suddenly bob up to the surface in a rather inconvenient way. Bluey smiled. He liked this man. Oink suggested that the usual way of "ballasting" an underwater pipeline was to construct it with concrete-clad steel pipes. The concrete gave additional stiffness and weight to the pipe and also protected the steel pipe from minor impact damage. Bluey knew what was coming next.

Simon W. Pain

"There doesn't seem to be any evidence of the concrete jacket showing on the radiograph," declared the enigmatic professor.

Of course, that's why the images look so sharp, thought Bluey.

"Not only that," continued the professor, "but you would expect the pipeline wall thickness to show some sign of age and corrosion either inside or outside. These pipe walls look as though they have just come straight from the pipe mill." Oink asked what the purpose of the pigging had been. "Was it for product separation, or maintenance purposes?" Bluey said he thought that it was for separation. The professor commented that the design of the pig was consistent with product separation but there was a wide range of pig designs. In particular, the "intelligent" pigs used for maintenance checks and monitoring the thickness of pipe walls were much larger devices and were much more susceptible to getting stuck because of their length and weight. He would send Bluey an email with attachments showing the different types of pigs and how they differed.

When the professor asked how the stuck pig had been found, Bluey confirmed that a radio-isotope "tracer" had been placed on the pig. Oink was puzzled, because he would have expected to see the radioisotope tracer showing clearly as a large white area on the radiograph, since that area would be over-exposed. The image in question had no indication of the presence of the isotope. The professor had just one last question. "Are you sure that this radiograph came from the Duroc pipeline, or could it have come from somewhere else?"

Bluey thanked the professor, replaced the phone, and sat back in his chair with his hands clasped behind his head. What if Oink was right, and the radiograph of the Duroc pipeline had somehow been substituted? He looked again at the image. The professor *was* right—everything looked a bit too pristine to be a

Duroc

radiograph of a pipeline that had been on the seabed for many years, and there was definitely no sign of a concrete jacket or of the radio-isotope. But who could have substituted a radiograph showing the right date stamp, and why would they want to do that?

Caitlin had just finished speaking on the phone, making arrangements for their trip to the *Merganser*. "We're both booked on a Sikorsky from Aberdeen the morning after tomorrow," she told Bluey. "I've also booked a couple of hotel rooms at Dyce near Aberdeen for tomorrow evening. We could drive up together after work tomorrow."

Then Bluey told Caitlin about the enigmatic Professor Oink. She giggled at the name.

"The professor's suggesting that the radiographic image might have been substituted, but I can't think why anyone would want to do that," Bluey said. "Would you please find out what you can about the incident with the diving bell on the *Merganser* before we travel? I'll start compiling the factual elements of the report about the crane incident on the GG."

It would be a while yet before he could write his conclusions and recommendations.

*****

Bluey stood by his car in the ground-floor car park of the uninspiring Ashe offices. He was about to set off for Aberdeen in preparation for the flight to the *Merganser*. He looked back and saw the staff doorway burst open and Caitlin emerged in her orange overalls emblazoned with the Ashe monogram. A little-used, pristine white hard hat was tucked under her arm and the soft curls of her long blond hair flounced as she walked. She looked stunning. Bluey thought she could have been gracing a cat walk, rather than crossing a tawdry commercial car park. Bluey smiled a welcome and took Caitlin's case and hard hat, which he placed in the boot. He held open the car door for his junior, and in no time they were headed across the aging Kincardine Bridge over the Firth of Forth, going north.

After discussing the usual niceties of how Bluey's boys were getting on at school and Caitlin's penchant for concerts that featured pop groups Bluey had never even heard of, the conversation inevitably returned to the common denominator of work and project enigma.

"Why would anyone want to substitute an image of a pipeline pig?" asked Caitlin again.

"There must be something about the original pig that someone doesn't want us to know."

"Maybe it's some new technology they've developed that they don't want their competitors to know about."

"Who're 'they'?" queried Bluey.

"Could be anyone."

"No. Not anyone. Remember, there are some common factors. Where has the pig come from?"

"Gannet Gamma."

"Who is the owner?"

"Duroc Offshore."

"And where is the pig headed?"

"Duroc Petrochemicals. I see what you're saying."

"You have to admit that all the incidents in the last few weeks seem to come back to the Duroc installations."

The discussion then moved back to the question of why someone would not want Ashe to know about the stuck pig.

As they drove north towards Dundee, they brainstormed ideas. The new pigging technology option didn't seem to be likely. The developer of a new pig could easily have come to Ashe and asked for confidentiality, and it almost certainly would have been granted. Caitlin queried whether there could be something else in the pipeline, instead of a pig. They thought that was unlikely; otherwise, it would have blocked the pipe near the rig and not travelled nearly 60 miles along the USP1 pipeline. But why was someone trying to put them off the scent? It now looked as though the radiograph of the pig that they had been sent was not the radiograph of the actual stuck pig. It was now obvious to them both that the image was far too distinctive and that there was no evidence of the concrete insulation. Nor did the image that they had been sent include the image of the section of pipe where the pig was apparently stuck. Someone was trying to interfere with their Project Enigma investigations. The real question was—why?

They drove in silence for a while. Caitlin suddenly sat up. "When I was very small, we had a shop in our town which had a pneumatic system that blew small cash-containing pods around the store. The sales assistant put a bill with your money into the pod and it shot off somewhere, and a few minutes later it came back with your change. They were like little pipeline pigs. What if our pig is transporting money, without anyone knowing it!"

Bluey looked across at her in astonishment, and for a little too long, because the car in front suddenly slowed down to take a left turn and Bluey very nearly ran into the back of it. It took him a moment to recompose himself and apologise. "Sorry about that! But you are right—the pig must be carrying something valuable!" He added "But why would you go to the trouble of using a pipeline pig to transport it? It must be something that needs to avoid customs—something small enough to fit in the pipe, something very valuable…"

"You mean like diamonds?"

"Yes, something small and valuable like that would fit the bill. You wouldn't want other people to know if you had taped a few sparklers to the pig, would you? Provided that the pig didn't get stuck, no one would ever know."

"But the pig transportation system did get stuck."

Simon W. Pain

"Exactly, and now it looks as though someone is starting to panic. What's more, if there is something unusual attached to the pig, then the technicians who load the pigs into the traps must know something about it. What did they call those pigging contractors on GG?"

"Scottish Pipeline Services."

"That's them. I think that Scottish Pipeline Services are due a visit. I'll need to check where they're based."

And with that, they found that it was now dark, and that they'd already passed Dundee and were on the long slog up to Aberdeen. They drove the rest of the way in thoughtful silence.

They checked in at the Drovers Inn on the outskirts of Aberdeen just after 8 p.m. that evening. After a pleasant and very casual meal in the bar, they arranged to meet up for breakfast at 7 o'clock the following morning. Then Bluey withdrew to phone home and catch up on some outstanding emails.

Bluey's room was quite basic, with rather ageing furnishings, but it was warm, clean, and comfortable. He sat on the bed with his laptop and started to review the usual email overload. Why did so many people copy emails to the whole world, when they were not relevant to you? He found the challenge was spotting the important messages. Amongst this latest consignment of trivia, he spotted one from Professor Oink. The message was very concise—it said "Fyi" and clearly had an attachment. Bluey downloaded the attachment and found that it was the promised document summarising the different type of pipeline pigs.

The first part related to the types of pigs that were used to separate different products. There was nothing very surprising there, although the detailed diagrams were very helpful to Bluey's understanding. He then moved on to the maintenance and inspection pigs. It seemed that these were the most commonly used. They varied quite a bit. One type was made of plastic foam and was shaped a bit like an artillery shell. These were the cheap and cheerful ones that were used for cleaning dirty pipelines. It was very noticeable from the diagrams that as the maintenance pigs became more sophisticated, they increased dramatically in length. Some of these were described as "intelligent" pigs. They housed lots of electronics, recorders, and batteries to enable the pig to use ultrasonic detectors to monitor the thickness of the pipe walls. This was obviously very important for buried or submerged pipes, which were difficult to visually inspect. The key point from a safety point of view was to identify when a pipeline was corroding, well before it sprang a leak or exploded. The blurb with the intelligent pigs suggested that because these pigs contained a lot of kit, it was sometimes necessary for the pig to be composed of more than one pig unit, coupled together in an articulated pig "train." The benefit of this was that the pig train was more flexible, and could negotiate bends more easily, than a single very long pig.

A light came on in Bluey's head. Caitlin and he had assumed that the stuck Duroc pig was a fairly standard product separation pig. What if it had been a much longer maintenance pig? Could that explain why the pig had got stuck? It had never occurred to them to ask if the location of the stuck pig was on a bend in the pipe. His mind was racing. He sprang up and dashed out of the door to hammer on Caitlin's door. She was in a white hotel robe and opened the door cautiously, not knowing who it could be. Bluey burst in, completely unaware that Caitlin was ready for bed.

"Look at this!" he said. "I've just been reading an email from Professor Oink, and the pigs can be much bigger than we thought!" Bluey sat down on the bed, put the laptop down on the bedside table, and waved his hands at the screen in excitement. "What if our pig is longer than we thought and is on a bend in the pipeline?"

Caitlin was standing, to avoid sitting on the bed beside Bluey. "Would it get stuck?" she said.

"I don't know, but it *is* possible, isn't it?"

"Well, if it's bigger than we thought, it might also carry diamonds the size of rocks." She gesticulated with her hands, emphasising how big the diamonds might be. "That would make it worthwhile for somebody."

Bluey suddenly realised the awkwardness of the situation. Caitlin had been about to go to bed and he had just blundered into her room. He needed to withdraw. The discussion could wait until breakfast. He mumbled an apology and clumsily returned to his own room in haste.

Chapter 15

The helicopter flight to the *Merganser* was Caitlin's first, and happily it went without her needing to resort to her helicopter underwater escape training. It was late morning when the Sikorsky floated down onto the helipad above the bridge of the *Merganser*. As Caitlin and Bluey climbed down the metal stairway to the bridge, they passed a line of crew members who stood back to let them into the bridge. Bluey thought that he recognised one of them. He paused for a minute and gave a smile of recognition. The crewman turned away. Then Bluey remembered. "Hello, Stylo," he said. Stylo gave a growl and looked up. "Did you do the radiography on the USP1 pipeline a few days ago?" asked Bluey.

"We don't do radiography," snarled Stylo and left. Bluey looked quizzically at Caitlin. That was not the answer he had expected or wanted. They moved on into the bridge to meet Findlay Innes, the master. After a short welcome, during which it was clear that Innes was not exactly pleased to see them, they were shown to their accommodation by the dive supervisor. It seemed that he was to be their main contact. As they wound their way through the maze of accommodation, Bluey said, "Was it Scottish Pipeline Services who carried out the radiography last week?"

"No, they don't do much radiography," said the dive supervisor. "We usually use I.R.L.—Industrial Radiography Ltd. They did the work last week. Jock McKee was the lead radiographer. We have used him before and he is very reliable. He is also the guy who was injured in the diving bell incident last week."

"Is he OK now?" asked Bluey.

"Yes. It seems he was concussed when the Liberty—I mean the diving bell—came off the hoist cable. He was medevac'd to Aberdeen Royal Infirmary as a precaution, but I gather he is OK."

"Were there any other radiographers in the bell?"

"There was a new man. I'd never seen him before. Think his name was something like Bogie. I don't know what his surname was. The change of personnel was very last minute. We didn't know this Bogie guy was coming until he stepped off the chopper."

"Did you get a copy of the radiographic image that they took?"

"I saw it, but the original must have been taken back to I.R.L."

"What can you remember about the radiographic image? Could you see the pig?"

By this time, they were outside the cabins that had been allocated to the visitors. The dive supervisor obviously didn't want to talk further. As Bluey stepped into his cabin, he whispered to Caitlin that he was going to phone I.R.L.

Meanwhile, Caitlin decided to take a walk to the dive control room. She introduced herself and asked if they had a map of the USP1 pipeline. The control room operator brought up a copy of the pipeline route on the computer screen. The scale was so small as to be unhelpful. Basically, the pipeline appeared to follow a straight line from the rig to the shore. She asked the operator if he could show a larger scale drawing of where the *Merganser* was on the map at the moment. He entered some co-ordinates and the map scrolled to a new position and then

Duroc

zoomed in to show a close-up of the line representing the pipeline. Now it was not absolutely straight, but showed a small dog-leg in the route.

"Is this where the pig is stuck?" she asked, pointing at the cranked section of the pipe. The operator said he thought it was. Anticipating Caitlin's next question, he explained that sometimes there were difficult features on the seabed that required the pipeline route to be altered, to avoid these obstacles. It looked as though there might be such a minor diversion here. Caitlin smiled at the breakthrough, thanked the operator and headed back to her cabin.

Bluey sat on the narrow bunk and connected to the ship's Wi-Fi. He soon found a phone number for Industrial Radiographics Ltd. He introduced himself to the operations manager and explained that they were investigating the causes of a diving bell failure on a diving vessel in the North Sea. He explained that the radiograph that Ashe had received from their radiographer didn't seem to be what he expected. In particular, he thought that the radiograph didn't show the concrete cladding around the pipe. The I.R.L. operations manager asked for the radiographic image to be e-mailed to him. In no time at all, he was back on the phone. It was clear that the image that had been sent to Ashe must have been sent in error, because that image was not the one taken of the USP1 with the stuck pig. However, the time stamp reference on the image did appear to be correct. The ops manager thought it was clear that this wasn't just an error, but had been done intentionally. Bluey asked how that could be, because he had received the image directly from the I.R.L. radiographer who had taken the image. The manager replied that there were two radiographers involved in taking the image. He said that Jock McKee had been the lead, but he was also the one who'd been injured in the diving bell incident. His partner was a new employee, who'd been contracted at short notice, just to do this job. He couldn't remember his name, but he could find out. In any case, as his employment had been for a single task, he had now left I.R.L. It had clearly been left to the second radiographer to e-mail the image to Ashe. Bluey thanked the operations manager and asked if he could send the correct image of the pig.

Bluey went next door to Caitlin's cabin. She was quite excited and told him what she'd found out from the dive control room operator. Bluey smiled and opened up his laptop. Just as he did, he was confronted by a message stating, "You've got mail." He opened the email, which was from I.R.L., and its attachment. Caitlin leaned across him with a waft of perfume. The screen showed a slightly fuzzy image of a long pig in a section of pipe. The time stamp was familiar. It was the same number as on the earlier image, but this was quite definitely a different image. Bluey pointed at the bright white lines designating the pipe walls. He pointed to the outer edge of the pipe wall, which showed a less dense, greyer area. It was clearly some sort of cladding. It could be concrete. The centre of the image was difficult to see because of a large white ball, like sunlight, obliterating everything in the centre of the picture. "And that's the radio-isotope tracer that we were expecting to see!" said Bluey triumphantly. In any normal-sized pig, all the detail would have been eradicated, but as this pig was so long, the cups at each end were still visible. One of the leading cups had become loose, resulting in the cup becoming jammed against the lower wall of the pipe. This, together with the fact that, as Caitlin had imagined, the pipe had a slight bend in it, had obviously caused the pig to come to a halt.

"Look at what you can see of the section between the cups. What would you expect to see?" said Bluey. Caitlin leaned forward. More perfume aroma. Although much of the centre section of the pig was visually obliterated, she could see the ends of

Duroc

some sort of cylindrical shape next to the cups. She said she thought it looked solid. Bluey replied that he wasn't sure it was solid. It was uniformly dense, yes, but he would have expected to see evidence of some electronic gadgetry. What was clear to him was that this pig would not have been capable of carrying out any sort of intelligent inspection, since it had no electronics. He suggested that this pig was the sort of illicit freight carrier they'd imagined earlier. "But it doesn't look as though it's carrying money, and if it is diamonds, then you and I are made for life, because the Cullinan Diamond is the world's biggest diamond so far, at about four inches long, and this is orders of magnitude bigger! No, I suspect it is not diamonds, but I do suspect some sort of smuggling operation. If you could put something into the pipeline at GG, then you could send it to the mainland without having to trouble the government with all the bureaucracy of paying duty! And if it's something that is inherently illegal, it's an even better scam!"

They needed to find out what the pig was carrying. They both had a pretty good idea of what to expect. The problem was that Bluey needed to work on investigating the diving bell failure incident. He suggested that he concentrate on that, whilst Caitlin could start to probe around and see what she could find about the pigging activity.

*****

Moura was not a happy man. They had found the pig. He had thrown Ashe off the scent by arranging for a phony radiograph, but it would only be a matter of time before they realised. Stylo had told him that on GG they were planning to bypass the stuck pig, and the equipment and resources to do that were being sent out to the dive ship at the moment. Once the section containing the pig was cut out and brought to the surface, they would be rumbled. So far, he thought that no one was suspicious of the pig or even knew of its cargo. However, that could soon change. The best thing that could happen was that the piece of cut pipe and its entombed pig would remain in Davy Jones's locker ad infinitum. It would be very expensive for him to write off the cargo, but it was the best solution in the long run. He needed a plan to ensure that the stuck pig never saw the light of day again. It would require more of his men on the *Merganser*. He would tell Stylo to get a couple more saturation divers out to the vessel. The ship's crew would need a lot of divers to carry out the by-pass work, because the work would go on around the clock. The challenge was going to be how to ensure that his men were the ones that actually carried out the final cut in the pipe that exposed the pig. He would speak to Stylo about it.

If Moura was unhappy, then Stylo was totally depressed. The scheme had been a great money spinner for him when things had been going well, but now it seemed that Murphy's Law had taken control and if anything could go wrong, it already had! Stylo listened as patiently as he could to Moura's rantings, but he already had his own, better plan. Moura didn't understand the practicalities. When cutting the pipeline underwater there was a risk of either leaking 60 miles worth of oil or gas into the sea, or, alternatively, filling the pipe with seawater—or both. To avoid this happening, it would be necessary to carry out what was known in the industry as a "hot tap and stopple" operation. The "hot tap" involved welding a large branch onto the pipeline and then using a special trepanning cutter through the branch to cut a hole in the main pipeline inside the branch. The cutter could then be removed, the branch isolated, and all the contents of the pipeline would remain inside the pipe. Then, in order to safely cut the main pipe, a special stopple device could be attached to the new branch, which, through the use of special levers, would allow a stopper to be

Duroc

inserted into the main pipe. This would have to be done on either side of the pig, and then the pig and a short section of pipe could be removed without all the contents from the pipeline spilling out into the water. It also had the advantage that once the section of pipe containing the pig was removed, a new section could be welded in place, without the need for a temporary by-pass pipe. It sounded easy, but it was an incredibly difficult series of tasks, even when you were working on dry land and not constrained by diving gear. The reason why Stylo was so keen on the idea, was that, although there was a reasonable supply of individuals who could carry out the welding, the trepanning and the stopple operations required very specialised equipment. There were only two companies in Scotland that had both the equipment and the expertise to carry out such work. The name of one of those companies was Scottish Pipeline Services Ltd.

*****

Bluey spent two full days examining every inch of the Liberty diving rig. Unfortunately, much of the detailed evidence relating to the incident had disappeared because the hoist cable and umbilical had been re-attached, the interior had been cleaned up and the ceiling grill replaced. The investigation was limited to a visual inspection of the bell, and interviews with the permanent ship's crew members. No interview was possible with the radiographers, as both men had left the *Merganser*, and their radiographic sources had likewise been returned to their base. The dive supervisor's records confirmed the training and qualifications of the radiographers, and their names were recorded as Jock McKee and his temporary partner Fergus Biggart. They said that, for some reason, the second radiographer had called himself Bogie, but they hadn't understood why. None of them had met Biggart before, and they commented that he'd had little to say for himself. Bluey noted that Biggart had joined the ship at very short notice after Jock's usual partner had been injured in the hit and run accident. That was interesting, but not directly relevant to the cause of the Liberty incident.

Discussions with the dive maintenance team showed that the main hoist cable had been replaced recently, following a routine inspection, and the radiographic dive had been the first occasion on which the new cable had been used. In the discussions it was suggested that the D-shaped shackle that connected the cable to the bell had become unscrewed, but that couldn't be definitely confirmed, because the remains of the shackle had fallen off and been lost somewhere in the depths of the North Sea. However, Bluey concluded that for the shackle to come loose, the locking device on the shackle pin must have been either loose or not fitted. He thought that the underlying cause of the incident was therefore that checks had not been carried out to ensure that the connection between the cable and the bell could not accidentally come apart.

But the failure of the hoist had not been the only problem. It seemed that the dive supervisor's decision to continue trying to lift the diving bell using the umbilical cord had been a further mistake. This had inevitably led to the failure of the cord and associated electric cables. It was a stroke of luck that Bogie had realised what had happened and been able to plug the air leak in the top of the bell chamber. If he had not done so, most of the air would have been released from the bell, allowing it to start to flood. Bluey thought that this would almost certainly have led to fatalities. He did praise the rescue squad in the Big Ben bell for their prompt and decisive action. It was largely through their actions that both Jock and Bogie had been rescued alive.

Duroc

Bluey reported back to Findlay, the ship's master, about his findings, and told him that the official report into the incident would follow in a few weeks' time.

Meanwhile Caitlin was learning to find her way around the ship and trying to find out what she could about the pigging. She already knew from Iain, the plant engineer at Duroc Petrochemicals, that the records of the recent pigging runs were either limited or non-existent. Add to that the fact that someone was trying to disguise whatever it was that the stuck pig was carrying—something that was probably illegal—and it all started to have a very bad smell. Her attempts to get information out of the crew members of the *Merganser* were not proving to be very successful. That was hardly surprising because the crew were only chartered to find the lost pig and then remove it. They had played no part in putting the pig into the pipeline. The only link that she could find to the *Merganser* consisted of the two radiographers from I.R.L. Neither of them was still on board—one was still in hospital and the other had disappeared. She would talk to Jock McKee by the ship-to-shore phone later, but she was suspicious about the other man, this Fergus (alias Bogie) Biggart. She talked to the operators in the dive control room. They all knew Jock well and seemed to speak highly of him. The other man was a complete stranger to them. They repeated the little she already knew about how Bogie had arrived at the *Merganser*. It was either a complete coincidence or very suspicious that one of the two regular radiographers should suddenly have had a road traffic accident, just when he was needed on the *Merganser*. She made a note to talk to the Scottish Police about the circumstances surrounding that accident.

She sauntered around the deck. It was a hive of activity. As she looked out over the ship's rail, she could see another rig support vessel starting to approach the *Merganser*. She climbed the ship's superstructure to get a better look. The other ship was manoeuvring very close to the *Merganser*. It looked as though she was coming in alongside, and the activity of deck hands on both ships reinforced the conclusion that something was about to happen. As the ship came slowly closer and closer, Caitlin could read the name. It announced that she was the *Rig Maiden* from Amsterdam. Caitlin stayed where she was and watched as the crew of the *Rig Maiden* dropped fenders over her rails that would cushion the two steel hulls. The water between the two ships was now frothing violently as both hulls made contact with the fenders, and crewmen hurriedly threw light hand lines to each other, before pulling across the main hawsers and tying them off.

The cargo deck of the *Rig Maiden* was full of assorted engineering equipment. Caitlin recognised the pre-prepared sections of pipes and crates of miscellaneous tools, but there was a large structure near the stern that she didn't recognise. It wasn't part of the ship, that was clear, but it looked like a rather strange steel shed. Caitlin turned to head down the stairway to the *Merganser*'s deck. She decided she would find out more about how the hyperbaric chambers worked, in order to keep the divers at a constant pressure and able to enter and leave the diving bells without de-pressuring.

She found one of the female technicians and introduced herself. The technician happily explained that the pressurisation chambers and the bells were filled with a helium-oxygen mixture known as Trimix. Apparently, this was not to be confused with the drug of similar name which was used to deal with problems of impotence! She pointed to a series of pipes and valves below the chambers. Those were the valves controlling the air mixture that came into the chambers. They went below the deck and Caitlin was shown another series of pressure vessels, in which the diving air was stored. She was told that as helium is expensive it was recovered from the divers'

Duroc

exhaled air and recycled. Caitlin found that fascinating. The technician also mentioned that the diving mixture could also be used in the habitat. Caitlin frowned. She didn't understand. The helpful technician asked if Caitlin had seen what had just arrived on the *Rig Maiden*. Apparently, the shed-like structure that Caitlin had seen on the deck of the *Maiden* was the habitat. It was going to be used to allow divers to work on the pipeline whilst they were underwater. It worked based on a principle that was similar to that used in the diving bells, but the habitat would become a temporary workshop on the seabed. All this was way beyond Caitlin's experience, and she suspected that that would be true for Bluey, too.

As it was starting to get late, Caitlin headed back into the accommodation section of the *Merganser*, to look for the galley.

Bluey was already there, getting stuck into a rather large T-bone steak. Caitlin joined him at the small yellow formica table. Her salad looked rather uninspiring opposite his feast. She told Bluey about the arrival of the *Rig Maiden*. He'd seen it, but had not understood the significance of the large shed on its deck. Caitlin showed off her new-found knowledge by telling him that it was a habitat, and it was to be used to allow work to be done on the pipeline. Bluey's eyebrows rose—he was clearly impressed by his young protégée. She also suggested that they should contact the police to find out more about the road traffic accident which had allowed the radiographer called Bogie to be substituted at short notice. They both suspected that Bogie was responsible for Ashe receiving the wrong radiograph. As they finished their meal chatting about the diving bell incidents, the surly character at the next table inexpertly twirled his Rubik's cube, before deciding that Moura needed to know about Ashe's suspicions.

Simon W. Pain

The Ashe investigators stayed on the *Merganser* for another 24 hours. Bluey concentrated on finding out more about the diving bell incident, whilst Caitlin was more interested in observing what was happening on the *Rig Maiden*. The habitat was being prepared for offloading, but it seemed that it would be lowered to the depths directly from the *Maiden*, because the stern hoists on the *Merganser* could not take the weight. The umbilicals, supplying services to the habitat, would be connected to the *Merganser*, to allow for diving controls to be carried out from there and so that the *Rig Maiden* could return to port or other duties. All the pipework and fittings had already been transferred directly to the deck of the *Merganser*.

A number of the crates carried the words "Scottish Pipeline Services." During the day, Caitlin left her surveillance of the ship's offloading and went to call Aberdeen police headquarters, to find out more about the road traffic accident that had prevented the original radiographer from attending. It turned out that she was right. It had been a hit and run. The sergeant who was investigating the incident had been convinced that it had been intentional. Unfortunately, he didn't have many leads in the investigation, as the other vehicle involved, a Volvo, had been reported stolen about an hour and a half before the collision. However, it was obvious that it had not been a casual bump, because the radiographer's car had been forced off the road at a bend in a heavily wooded area. The radiographer's injuries were serious, and the accident and emergency department at Aberdeen Royal Infirmary had confirmed that the injuries were consistent with the car crashing into trees. The sergeant confirmed that the stolen Volvo that was thought to be the cause of the collision had been found burnt out on derelict land on the outskirts of Peterhead. The sergeant said that what was significant was that, despite the radiographer's car having crashed into trees, it had bumps on the rear bumper and boot that were consistent with it having been "shunted." He also noted that although all the paintwork and DNA evidence on the burned-out Volvo had been erased by the fire, there were signs of damage to the front of that vehicle. The only problem was that he didn't know who the perpetrator was, or even what the motive might be.

Caitlin explained that she thought the motive was to get a different radiographer onto the *Merganser*. She explained the background and suggested that the person responsible for the collision could be a man known as Fergus Biggart, or one of his associates. It seemed that his nickname was "Bogie." The sergeant thought for a moment, and then he said that if that was the man's real name, he shouldn't be too difficult to find, because North Sea divers had to go through all sorts of regulatory and training checks. He thanked Caitlin for her help and said that they should "stay in touch."

Caitlin found Bluey and told him that it looked as though this Bogie had got himself purposely onto the radiography team looking for the stuck pig. After some discussion, Bluey said that he planned to go over to the GG rig whilst he was here, ostensibly to finish off the investigation into the crane incident, but also to ask a few pertinent questions about the pigging operation. Given that Caitlin had had the warning at the helicopter escape training about not returning to the GG, Bluey suggested that she return home and said that he would take a boat over to the GG on his own.

Chapter 16

Caitlin took an uneventful chopper flight back to Dyce the following morning. Life returned to its usual drudgery of sorting out domestic chores and catching up on routines in the Ashe office. There had been no new reports of incidents or accidents to investigate, so she concentrated on completing the outstanding bellows incident report at Duroc Petrochemicals. It turned out that Clare Maxwell, who had been injured in the explosion, was now out of hospital, and that her colleague, Steve Bass was fully recovered. The plant was fully repaired but couldn't restart because it had run out of feedstock on account of the stuck pig. There had to be some link between what had happened at the petrochemicals plant that Duroc owned and its rig operations, but she couldn't work out what it was.

As she was browsing her way through the various witness statements on the computer screen she found herself looking at the record of the discussion with Carl Dunne, the technician who had been asked to inspect the ill-fated bellows. Carl had said that he had worked on both the GG rig and the Duroc Petrochemicals plant. He'd said that he seemed to think that he had previously heard the voice that had instructed him to inspect the bellows. What's more, he'd said that he thought he had heard that voice when he was on the GG. Was there something here? She picked up the phone and called Martyn Southwick, the safety manager at the Duroc Plant. It appeared that

Duroc

Carl had been talking to Martyn about the incident and had remembered something else: the name of the person who'd told him to urgently do the bellows inspection. The name was "Moura."

Martyn confirmed that there was no one by that name at Duroc Petrochemicals. Caitlin thanked him and immediately rang Duroc Offshore's Gannet Gamma rig. Again, she drew a blank. She was told there were no employees on the GG by that name. Who was Moura? She was fiddling pensively on her computer keyboard and inadvertently typed "MOURA" into Google. She got immediate responses:

"Moura: Also known as Estrela, Mouro and Pereira. A <u>PIG</u> breed originating from Canastra, Canastrao and also <u>DUROC</u> in southern Brazil."

She dropped the remains of her paper coffee cup in astonishment and a wet brown stain started oozing over her desk. In a panic she grabbed an old scarf from the back of her chair to mop up the spillage before it did any damage. This had to be significant. Everything seemed to relate to pigs. And she was convinced that it wasn't the animal variety. The company's names were based on pigs and now, it seemed, so was the name of the key man. The only thing was, she thought that Moura was probably an alias, so it could be almost anyone. However, this did confirm that the stuck pig in the USP1 pipeline must be really significant! She was convinced the pigs were being used for some major illicit activity. It might have been going on for some time, but the fact that the pig had got stuck would clearly be a major problem for Mr Moura. Once the pig was removed from the pipeline, the game could be up.

She wasn't going to solve that today, but she rang Bluey on the GG rig to tell him what she had found. Bluey was still out on the rig structure, and so she left an answerphone message that was transferred to the *Merganser*. Feeling that she had had a really successful day, she left the office early on the Triumph and decided on an early night.

Sunday morning came and it was time for the early morning run at the Kelpies again. She jogged round her usual 5 km route in the half light, ending up beside the massive silver sculptures. There, as usual, was the vagrant. But his demeanour was anything but normal. Caitlin was about to pass on by, when she noticed that the dishevelled figure didn't appear to be moving. She slowed to a walking pace, looking around for any other sign of assistance. There was none. She cautiously approached the prone body and knelt down beside it, searching for vital signs. Suddenly, from behind her, a rough hand grabbed across her mouth. It stifled her scream. There was an overwhelming smell of ether. Caitlin was not one to give up. She wriggled and thrashed about, trying to get free. She was on her knees beside the vagrant, with her assailant behind her. With all her strength she suddenly straightened both legs and shot upwards and backwards, at the same time biting the hand across her mouth. She drew blood. The assailant was thrown off balance for a moment. His hand and the ether gauze were thrown away from her face. She was free. She started to run away from her assailant, who was sprawling on his back behind her, nursing his bitten hand. The assailant yelled, "Stop the bitch!" At that instruction, the apparently comatose vagrant sprang miraculously to life and gave chase. Caitlin was running as fast as she could past the sculptures, yelling "Help!" at the top of her voice. Only two people heard her screams, and neither of them were going to help! Caitlin was younger and fitter than the "vagrant," and she had a head start on both of her pursuers. There were only the massive Kelpie sculptures to act as a refuge, and so she ran behind one of the huge stainless steel horses' heads. Flattening

Duroc

herself against the cold steel she chanced a look back and saw the vagrant bent double, his hands on his knees. He obviously didn't work out in the gym! But the other assailant, a tall man in a black balaclava ski mask and tight-fitting jumpsuit, was back on his feet and heading her way. She sidled around the back of the sculpture, staying out of sight of her hunters. Suddenly she noticed a man walking a dog, coming towards the water pools by the sculptures. Her hunters would also see him in a minute. Could she use him to help? She called out to him as loudly as she dared. The deaf man never heard her, but the hunters did! Their problem was that now there was someone else there—they couldn't just snatch the girl, and soon the tourists would be coming. They walked towards the dog walker, removing their facial coverings as they did so. The unshaven one spoke to the dog walker. No reply. He repeated his comment and the dog walker looked blankly at him and shrugged, pointing to both ears. "Can't hear," he mouthed.

"He's deaf!" said the vagrant and dragged the unshaven one away.

By this time the girl had vanished. She had made it unseen to the second Kelpie structure—the one where the horse's head is looking up to the sky. She was breathing heavily. As she sidled around the large base, she noticed a door in the side. She pressed on the door but it didn't open. The latch was on the inside. There was a stick about two yards away. Would they see her if she went for the stick? She picked up a large stone and threw it in the opposite direction. As the stone hit the ground, her hunters looked in its direction. That gave her the chance to grab the stick. She rushed back to the door with it, thrust it through a gap in the sculpture cladding, and managed to raise the latch. The door burst open and she slipped inside.

The inside of the sculpture consisted of a rather randomly shaped steel structure which provided the support for the stainless-steel jigsaw cladding. Caitlin immediately started to clamber up the structure towards the horse's nose. Dawn was still breaking outside, but the sculpture was made of a loosely fitting jigsaw of stainless-steel pieces. It was like being inside a giant colander. As she looked down from increasingly high vantage points, she could make out the silhouettes of her two hunters through the gaps in the sculpture's jigsaw. They were pacing around the base of her sculpture. She could hear their profanities when they couldn't find her.

Suddenly they had found the door. It was still latched, so they couldn't get in, but it wouldn't take them long to figure it out—it wasn't rocket-science. There was a click and the door burst open. Caitlin stopped climbing and froze, hardly daring to breathe. Her heart thumped in her chest, seeming to make a noise like a jackhammer. She flattened herself against the structure. Just at that moment, the rising sun caught the sculptures for the first time, and shafts of dappled orange light spread through the inside of the sculpture. Miraculously, the light created a camouflage effect, and even though the unshaven one looked up, he couldn't see the fugitive. The hunters looked around, muttered to each other and left. Caitlin was too scared to move. She stayed put, up amongst the jigsaw pieces of the structure, for what seemed like an eternity. There was no sign of the hunters prowling around the outside. Eventually, she started to cautiously make her way back down to ground level. When she was still about four metres above the ground, her foot slipped off the girder. She shrieked and a trainer clattered to the floor. She froze for the second time, staring at the trainer on the floor. The minutes passed and then the door was flung open and the unshaven one was back. He looked up and their eyes locked together. His lips split in an evil smirk. "Get down here," he ordered. "No" was her snapped reply.

Duroc

He didn't give her a second chance. He dashed out of the sculpture door and in no time was back with a red tube under his arm. "Switch on," snarled the unshaven one to his vagrant colleague. The fire hose under his arm sprang into life, and a jet of pressurised water shot up the inside of the sculpture, straight at Caitlin. The impact of the water knocked her off the steel girder. She caught hold of another girder and dangled under it, but her arms wouldn't hold on for long. And the pounding water was pulling her jogging bottoms around her ankles. After less than two minutes of this torture, her arms couldn't hold on any more, and with another scream her saturated body crumpled to the floor. The unshaven one sprang forward and suddenly Caitlin was aware of an overpowering smell of ether, but this time she had no energy to resist.

*****

Life on the MS *Merganser* was a hive of activity. The working habitat, which served as a sort of underwater repair shop, was in place on the seabed over the pipeline, and the *Rig Maiden* had returned to port. Arrangements were already in place to start welding the two new branches onto the pipeline adjacent to the location of the stuck pig. The plan had changed. It had been decided by the Gannet Gamma management that they would not by-pass the pig. They would simply cut out the damaged section of the pipe and lift it to the surface with the stuck pig still inside, then a replacement piece of pipe, which had been delivered to the *Merganser* from the *Rig Maiden*, could be welded in place. It sounded simple—definitely not! Two teams of saturation divers were already in the *Merganser's* hyperbaric pressurisation chambers, ready to start work on installing the two large branches for the hot tap and stopple operation. Duroc Offshore Ltd. had placed a contract with a specialist company to carry out the operation. The name of that specialist contractor was Scottish Pipeline Services Ltd.

The *Merganser* crew had already implemented the safety improvements to the diving bells that had arisen from Bluey's investigation, and one of the saturation diving teams was already making its way into the Big Ben diving bell, ready for the trip down to the habitat. There were three men: two diver welders and a bellman. Safety was being given a much higher priority following the incident on the Liberty diving bell. The umbilical and hoist shackle had been tested many times over, to ensure that there would be no further failures. If there were, someone would be held accountable at the next Sheriff's Fatal Accident Enquiry. The Big Ben was already being lowered into the water through the moonpool. The large pipe branches had already been delivered to the seabed, and so the first stage of the plan to remove the pig obstruction in USP1 was about to get underway.

When Big Ben reached the seabed, the two yellow-helmeted divers slipped out of the bell and waded their way across to the habitat access. They climbed up into the habitat, which was partially flooded with water. Before the fitting could start work, the branch would have to be fitted to the top of the pipeline. The end to be welded had already been shaped to match both the profile of the pipe wall and the requirements to get a reliably close-fitting weld. Positioning it would be easier with the habitat flooded, to get the benefit of additional buoyancy when lifting the branch into position. The concrete sleeve had already been cut back from the pipe and so, working in flooded conditions in the habitat, the two divers rigged up a hoisting device to lift the first branch on top of the pipeline. The divers used a wet welding technique to tack weld the branch in place. The thick stream of gas bubbles streaming from the welding torch shielded the electricity from being conducted through the water

Duroc

and harming the welder. They completed the lifting and tack welding of the two branches in a single work shift. The completion of the welding would be a much longer task, because in order to get a high-quality weld it would need to be done in the dry—what the divers called hyperbaric welding. The divers left the habitat and returned to the *Merganser*'s pressurised accommodation, using the Big Ben diving bell taxi service. In the meantime, in the control room, the dive supervisor started the process of remotely pumping out and blowing down the habitat to prepare a dry environment for the next team of divers to complete the welding in less demanding, or at least less wet, conditions.

Below the main deck of the *Merganser*, an orange-suited figure headed towards the valve station that Caitlin had been shown. The figure skilfully operated the manual valves to allow oxygen and helium to be blown down the umbilical cord to start the blowdown of the habitat. After about an hour of blowing down the habitat, the dive supervisor declared that the habitat was dry and ready for the back-up team of saturation divers to start work. This time they took the Liberty taxi down to the seabed and waded across to the habitat. When they entered the habitat, the air pressure was equalised, allowing them to surface into a relatively dry, albeit cold, space. Remarkably, considering the depth, they were able to remove their diving helmets and breath the air in the habitat. They reported to the bellman that they had entered the habitat and lost no time in starting to complete the welding of the branches. The welding needed to be of high quality and would have to pass stringent radiographic tests before the next stage of the work could proceed, and so it was slow progress, with the need to lay down several runs of weld metal to give the strength required. Once the branches were fully installed, they didn't want the palaver of returning to the depths to do it all over again! To avoid the problems of flash from the blue welding arc, which could seriously damage the retina of the eye, only one welder worked at a time, giving the other a few minutes' rest, or time to chip the slag from the weld.

The air in the habitat was becoming hazy with fumes and smoke, even though the air in the chamber was being circulated. For a moment, the blue welding arc died down and things went quiet. The diver who was not welding at the time looked across at his mate, assuming that he was stopping to change welding electrodes, but the welder just seemed to be weary. The resting diver called across to ask if he was OK. The other diver replied with the comical squeaky voice that was a consequence of breathing the diving air mixture that he was fine. The welding restarted, but now the non-welding diver started to feel odd. Initially it was just a tweak above the eyes, but then it quickly turned into a full-blown headache. He was aware of welding stopping. He looked again at his mate and saw him starting to slump against the pipeline. The diver realised what was happening: the oxygen levels were too low in the habitat and they were starting to be slowly asphyxiated. With great presence of mind, he managed to get to his diving helmet and start the flow of breathable oxygen. After a few minutes he began to regain his self-control.

He managed to crawl over and get his mate's diving helmet. He helped him put it on and started the flow of air. They both slumped against each other, back-to-back, for some time, until their senses returned sufficiently for them to contact the bellman. They were back to breathing 21% oxygen and so the immediate danger was past, but it was some time before they were able to return to the Liberty diving bell. This attempt at completing the welding of the pipeline branches was abandoned and the two divers and the bellman were returned to the pressurised chamber on the *Merganser* to recover.

Duroc

There was a short inquest in the dive control room about how the oxygen levels in the habitat had become low. The anxious dive supervisor went out to the valve station and found that the oxygen valve was not fully open. No one could explain why, but the supervisor reminded everyone of the importance of ensuring that the diving air was breathable. Lives depended on it. The incident was never reported to Ashe.

A full day later, the diving air was passed as breathable and the first team of divers returned to the habitat to complete the welding of the two branches.

A five-member team from Scottish Pipeline Services, together with their equipment, had been on board the *Merganser* since the *Rig Maiden* had arrived. Once the welding was completed, two radiographers from the diving team needed to go down to radiograph the new welds. Having been caught out once, Bluey had insisted that he was present when the radiographs were developed. He was on a boat returning from the GG at the time that the radiograph started, and so he was completely unaware of the two welders having nearly been asphyxiated. When he arrived back at the *Merganser*, there was an answerphone message waiting for him. It was an excited Caitlin, telling him what she had found out about someone by the name of Moura. It sounded significant. It was Monday and Caitlin should be in the office, so he called her. There was no reply—the phone went to the answering machine. Bluey called his boss and told him that he would be remaining on the *Merganser* for a little longer, until he could see the radiographs of the new branch welds. He went on to ask him to pass a message to Caitlin. "Caitlin's not in today," was the reply. Bluey frowned. He thought that was odd—she was usually very reliable—but he thought no more about it.

It took another 24 hours for the radiographs to be completed, brought to the surface and developed. Bluey was in the dive control room to see the first results. The welds on both branches looked remarkably good. What was more, Bluey could see the edge of one of the pig cups at the inner edge of the upstream branch. He was confident that it was a genuine radiograph this time. The next step was to pressure test the branches before cutting into the main pipeline. They needed to be doubly sure that none of the repairs would leak. Bluey took a copy of the radiographs and told the dive supervisor that he required to be present when the section of pipe containing the stuck pig was brought to the surface. Once that was agreed, Bluey took the next chopper flight back to Aberdeen.

It was still mid-afternoon when he flew into Aberdeen, so he collected his car and drove down the road towards Falkirk, arriving at the Ashe offices just as everyone else was leaving. He went to his desk just to drop off the radiographs, but as he entered the open plan office, his boss called to him. "Bluey, you need to hear this!"

Bluey stepped into his boss's office, which was half panelled with reeded glass.

"Listen to this," his boss said, gesticulating at the answerphone. "It was left earlier today." He switched on the phone recording.

They sat listening in horror to the short message. It was a husky man's voice speaking.

"We've got the girl. Back off the Merganser *investigation and don't go to the cops or it'll be the worse for her."* The man left no name or contact arrangements.

Bluey's mind was in a spin. The only girl related to the *Merganser* investigations was Caitlin. Did that mean that they had somehow got her—could she have been kidnapped? And who were "they"?

Duroc

His boss said that he had called Caitlin at home as soon as he'd heard the message, but there had been no answer. So far, he hadn't called the police. "What's going on, Bluey?"

Bluey brought his boss up to speed with what was happening in what he and Caitlin were calling "Project Enigma," and what Caitlin had found out about the mysterious Moura. If Caitlin had been abducted, then he thought it could be linked to this Moura character, but right now they had very little to help identify this man. Bluey suspected that he was somehow linked to the Duroc group of companies.

"You need to find Caitlin," said his boss. "It's too risky to involve the police at the moment."

"Got any bright ideas?" muttered Bluey to himself as he left the office.

*****

It was pitch black and very cold. Caitlin didn't know if that meant it was night, or just that there was no light. She was in a tiny, cramped space. Her breathing was irregular and she felt sick. The ether had knocked her out and she was having difficulty thinking clearly. How long had she been unconscious? She remembered that her hunters had been chasing her around the sculptures. She felt her clothes. They were cold and wet. A car door slammed and she felt the perimeter of her prison vibrate. She realised that she must be in the boot of a car. The engine started, brake lights flickered in her space, voices sounded in the car. There must be at least two men in the car. She tried to move and explore the limits of the boot, but her movement was constrained in all directions. She was trussed up inside some sort of a hessian sack. The good news was that at least she could breathe; the bad news was that her chances of escape were minimal. She was suddenly sick, making life inside the sack even worse. She didn't know what was happening. Her mind was still in a fog from the ether. She could hear mumblings from inside the car, but her brain couldn't rationalise the words. Where was she being taken? The car was gathering speed—it must be on a main road now. Who were they and why had she been taken whilst she was just jogging and offending nobody? Tears welled up in her eyes. A bit more wet didn't matter as she was still damp all over from the fire hose. The fire hose! She suddenly realised that this was not a random abduction. If you choose someone at random and they don't want to come, you don't flush them down with a fire hose, you go and find somebody else to abduct! It suddenly dawned on her that her kidnappers had known who they were looking for. They were looking for Caitlin. But why? What could she be worth to them?

The car drove for about another 15 minutes. Caitlin could see the back of the rear lights shining inside the boot. She guessed that it was dark now, but she had been out for a morning jog at the Kelpies! Where had she been for the last 12 hours? She felt around inside the sack and felt the smooth curve of her naked thighs—where were her jogging pants? So many questions with no answers.

The car had slowed now. The glow from the rear lights went out. Pitch black. The car door opened and she heard someone get out. A rattle of chains and the creak of a metal hinge in need of oiling. The car crept forward. They must be passing through a door or gate. The hinge creaked again, the door slammed and the car bounced forward. If they were inside a building, then the floor had been laid by a drunken labourer. No, she thought that they were on some sort of a rough track. She worried that would mean "remote." The car moved carefully forward and it seemed that it was still without lights. After a few minutes they came to a halt again. Two car doors opened. And she heard footsteps walking away from the car. Shortly the steps returned, accompanied by a sound of scraping tin. The footsteps were coming around to the back of the car. She heard a key

Duroc

slide into the boot lock. Caitlin froze. They were coming to get her! The boot popped open. The unshaven one spoke. "Grab the bag—looks like she's still out cold." Caitlin mimed death. She could hear sounds in the background. They seemed somehow familiar. She was plucked out of the boot and her forehead smashed against the boot lid. It felt like a knockout blow, but she daren't call out. With a dull thump which resounded through the air like a church bell on a quiet Sunday, her containment bag was dropped like a sack of potatoes onto a metal sheet.

"Sshh!" It was the vagrant. She recognised his voice. Then it seemed that the two abductors lifted the metal sheet that she had been unceremoniously dropped on. It curved around her aching body. She knew now that she was on a sheet of corrugated iron.

The two porters struggled to carry the tin tray and its cargo over what felt like very rough ground. Caitlin continued to feign death whilst listening to the background sounds that were punctuated by occasional expletives from her captors. They were climbing up some steps now. Not many, because very soon they were going down again. What were those sounds she could hear? Suddenly the corrugated iron sheet was dropped on the ground.

"I told yer to be quiet!" That must be the unshaven one speaking. "Get 'er out."

The top of her sack was ripped open. She got a short glimpse of where she was. But that glimpse was enough—she knew, and then that hand and gauze were over her face again. More ether—she sank into oblivion.

Chapter 17

Bluey was at home. Debbie immediately knew that something was wrong. He wasn't his usual chirpy self. Bluey wanted to tell her what had happened to Caitlin, but the more people who knew, the more dangerous it could turn out to be for Caitlin, so he kept quiet.

How do you find someone who has been abducted, without involving the police? If it was because of the stuck pig, then whoever it was, perhaps Moura, would know he was involved in the investigation and would make contact. He didn't even know where to start. He couldn't even see what the kidnappers would expect him to do. However, it was obvious that Caitlin had become a pawn in some sort of barter deal. Bluey didn't sleep at all that night. Debbie was a bit upset, because they would usually make love when Bluey returned from business nights away, but not tonight. He tossed and turned all night long. It didn't help—he had no clearer plan in the morning than he had had when he'd gone to bed.

After a sulky breakfast, he kissed Debbie and the boys and said that even though it was the weekend, he had to go back to work. Debbie gave him a load of ear-ache and disappeared to the kitchen without stopping to say goodbye.

He had no clear objective. He stopped the car and rang Caitlin's parents again. He had to be careful, because he didn't want to cause alarm. Mr Barland, Caitlin's dad, answered. Bluey

Duroc

explained that he was Caitlin's boss and that they had been working together on one of the North Sea ships. Caitlin had finished earlier than he and had returned home on Friday. Bluey apologised for calling on the week-end but there was something that he needed to talk to Caitlin about before he saw her at work on Monday. Caitlin's dad explained that she had had a busy week and so would be catching up on the household chores over the week-end, except when she went for her run, first thing on Saturday and Sunday mornings. Bluey forced himself to chat amiably and asked where she went for a run. It was always the same place. She went to the Helix Park beside the Kelpies. She always did about a 5 km run. Bluey thanked Mr Barland for his help and wished him a good weekend. What he really meant was that he hoped he could find his daughter alive before Mr Barland knew she was gone! But he drove past the Ashe offices and on to the Helix Park. He ambled across to the sculptures. A park warden was working alongside one of them, the one where the horse's head is looking to the sky. The warden was inside one of the sculptures coiling up a fire hose. Bluey stopped and spoke with him.

"It's the kids, they make such a mess," the warden said. "This morning they've been spraying water everywhere." Bluey passed on his sympathies. His boys wouldn't do that. Or he hoped they wouldn't! As the warden took the neatly coiled hose back to its fire box, Bluey offered to close the door, but it didn't latch. He opened it again to see what the problem was. The door was catching on a trainer lying on the floor. It was relatively new, but still soaking wet. Bluey picked up the trainer, lifted up the tongue and read a something written in blue biro. It said "Caitlin B."

Caitlin had been there that morning.

Bluey was galvanised. He caught up with the park warden and asked if he knew who was in the park early in the mornings. He confirmed that an attractive young girl with long golden hair in a ponytail was a regular jogger at about 7 a.m. on week-end mornings. Bluey thought that could be Caitlin. The warden went on to say that there were also quite a few dog walkers between 7 and 10 o'clock. "Oh, yes, there's always a vagrant who seems to stay most nights and leaves by about this time to beg in the town centre."

The vagrant wasn't there, but there were some dog walkers. Even though the timing was too late, Bluey sauntered over to one of the dog walkers. It was a lady with a fluffy labradoodle. She said she only came out at this time of the morning, because of getting the children's breakfasts, so she wouldn't have been around at dawn. Bluey asked if she knew any of the early dog walkers. She didn't.

He carried on walking around the sculptures, talking with anyone whom he thought might have been around earlier. Not many were early risers. He was about to give up when he met an elderly man in his 60s. He looked fit and had a black and white collie on one of those extending leads. The dog was starting to slow down, as if they had been out for a while. Yes, he had been out from about 8 a.m. today, but he hadn't seen anything untoward. Bluey explained that he was looking for an attractive young girl in her early 20s. No, the elderly man hadn't seen anything. Bluey was about to leave, when the man said, "Why don't you try him," pointing to a man sitting on a park bench about 50 yards away. "He spends a lot of time here, and gets here early. He might know something." Bluey said, "Thanks," and set off towards the bench. He had only gone a few yards when the elderly man called after him again. "I should have said—that guy, I think he's pretty deaf." Bluey waved and headed towards the apparently deaf man.

Bluey sat down on the bench, looked towards the deaf man, and smiled. The smile was returned. "Are you deaf?" The deaf

Duroc

man shook his head and cupped a hand to his ear, indicating that he was indeed deaf. Bluey shuffled up the bench towards the man, and took a piece of paper and pencil out of his pocket. He wrote "I'm looking for someone, and wonder if you could help." The man shrugged, but was still smiling. "Were you here in the park at 7 a.m.?" wrote Bluey. The man surprised Bluey when he spoke. It was with a bit of a lisp and in the way that is typical of those who have been deaf since birth. "Yeth," he said.

Bluey used paper and pencil to explain that he was looking for a young girl, in her 20s. The deaf man's face suddenly lit up. He was not speaking clearly, but it was obvious he had seen something. He took the paper and pencil and started writing. Bluey read the neat text. There had been a girl in a track-suit. She had been running around the Kelpies. She'd seemed scared. Two very rough looking men had approached him and said something, but of course he couldn't hear. Bluey asked what the men were like. He wrote that one looked like a tramp. He thought he had seen him here before. The other man was wearing a black jumpsuit. He thought that just before the man had spoken, he'd been wearing a balaclava-type ski mask, but he'd taken it off. Bluey wrote "Were they chasing the girl?" The deaf man wasn't sure. But they didn't look to be up to any good.

Bluey thanked the deaf man, patted his dog and was about to leave when the strange voice of the deaf man told him to wait. The deaf man was rummaging in the pocket of his coat. He took out a scrap of cigarette packet. He flipped open the top and there, in neat blue biro was scribbled a car registration number. "It'th the man'th—the one with the mathk." Bluey thanked him profusely, took the packet and ran to his car.

Had he got a registration number of the car that had abducted Caitlin?

Back at his car, Bluey rang his friend Sergeant Jim Crieff at the Scottish Police. Ashe had a close professional relationship with Jim, because it was sometimes necessary to be escorted by the boys in blue when visiting hostile employers. Bluey asked Jim if he could check a car number-plate for him. The number was SF 65 XHZ. Jim came back immediately. The car was stolen but hadn't yet been recovered. The owner lived just outside Falkirk, so Bluey decided to call in on the way back to the office. He might learn something of interest.

Less than five minutes later he parked outside a grey rendered bungalow in a rather nondescript street. He knocked at the door and it was opened by a dour Scot. His demeanour was not improved by the fact that apparently he'd just had his car nicked! He went on about it, ad nauseam. However, Bluey did manage to find out that the car was his pride and joy—an immaculate old type 28 Lotus Cortina in ermine white factory colours with a Sherwood green stripe. It featured a particularly large boot and a modern Satnav! In its hey-day, it had been capable of 108 mph. He had parked the car at the Howgate Shopping Centre on Saturday, to go to the post office. He'd only been gone for 10 minutes, and when he got back the car wasn't there. He was furious. However, he said that the one good thing about it was that there was virtually no petrol in it. He'd been planning to fill up as soon as he'd left the post office. He surprised Bluey by a seemingly out-of-character chuckle, at the thought of the thieves running out of petrol whilst being chased by the cops! The cops had said it was probably joy-riders and when the car ran out of fuel it would be found abandoned on derelict land somewhere. After what seemed like half an hour of haranguing, Bluey had had enough and managed to extricate himself from the doorstep and retreat to his car. He was exhausted and didn't seem to have found out very much other than that the former Lotus Cortina owner was quite angry. It had been a waste of time. As Bluey drove away, the curtains twitched and the old man gave a satisfied smirk.

Duroc

Bluey drove back home, but something about what the old "petrol head" had told him, didn't seem to make sense. He couldn't quite put his finger on it. He drove home only to find that Debbie and the boys had gone out. He suddenly realised that at the week-end he had been supposed to be taking the boys to Stenhousemuir for their football practice. Another black mark from Debbie, but he couldn't tell her about Caitlin yet—it would only lead to the police being drawn in. It was too late to go to the football now. He would just have to face the music when the time came. There would be a day of reckoning!

*****

She was sick again. Caitlin had no idea how long she had been comatose. Every part of her body ached. She wasn't sure whether the aches were from physical injury or just that she was so cold. It must still be night-time, though, because she couldn't see a thing. She was lying on some thick soft material, maybe a blanket or a jumper, or her own track-suit. She gingerly sat up with her eyes wide open, but was unable to see anything in the inky darkness. There was a strong smell, but she wasn't sure what it was. She carefully stretched a hand out, moving her arm in an arc above her head. She tried the other arm. Apart from the floor and blanket, her hands didn't touch anything. Her hands and arms were free, not tied up. She repeated the exercise with her legs. No ligatures there either. She knelt and tried to stand up. She felt upwards but couldn't feel a ceiling. Where was she? Could she have been dumped in a field in a very dark area? She looked up to see if there were stars, or the moon. Nothing but blackness. She slumped back to the floor and tried to wrap the blanket around herself to try and keep warm. She pondered her predicament. The two men and their car seemed to have gone. She said quietly, "Is anyone there?" Then slightly louder, "Is anybody there?" No answer.

Simon W. Pain

She was on her own, but where? She felt in her tracksuit top pocket—her phone was still there. Her abductors were so disorganised they had forgotten to check if she had a phone! She felt better and took the phone out, intending to call for help. In the pitch dark, she switched the instrument on. It wasn't her phone at all; it was a small walkie talkie. The men must have exchanged it for her phone. She panicked for a moment. After a few minutes she composed herself. She could understand why they would take her phone, but what was the purpose of the walkie-talkie? It could only be so that they could communicate with her, without being seen. She was tempted to try it. No, she would wait and try and find out more about where she was first. She clung on to the blanket and cautiously started to crawl. She had no idea where she was going or even in what direction. It was slow progress. It was agony on her knees. The floor seemed to be fairly flat, but covered by dry and dusty dirt. She scooped some of the dust up in her hand and put it to her nose. It had a rank and rusty smell. She crawled for what seemed like a quarter of an hour without finding any boundary wall. She changed direction and crawled for another quarter of an hour. Still no edge to her prison. She was getting desperate. She sat on the floor and took out the walkie-talkie. She would try and contact the kidnappers. She found and pressed the transmit button. "Can you hear me?" she called.

There was an immediate reply of unintelligible static. "I can't hear you." More static. It was hopeless. Clearly the kidnappers hadn't thought through the communications arrangements. She started to try and think of the possible reasons why the radio wouldn't work. It could be that the signal was too weak, or that the transmitting device was too far away, or... what about a Faraday cage? Caitlin remembered her school physics teacher talking about Faraday cages. She remembered that aeroplanes can be struck by lightning without being damaged or any of the passengers and crew being injured because the plane forms this Faraday cage. They were boxes that were made of metal that shielded certain types of electromagnetic radiation, and in particular radio waves. She thought of the smell of the dust and concluded she must be inside a huge metal box. The walkie-talkie was never going to work. Was that good news or bad news? If she was going to be imprisoned for some time, she would need food, at least.

Having wandered around for some time inside the box, she didn't know how to get back to where she had started. It didn't really matter. She lay down on the cold metal floor, wrapped the blanket tightly around her and cried herself to sleep.

*****

It was Monday morning. The weekend had been a disaster for Bluey. Debbie wasn't speaking to him, the boys didn't know what had gone wrong between Mum and Dad, and he had made little progress on finding Caitlin. He had set off early to the office, but changed his mind after only two miles and turned the car around, deciding to go to Duroc Petrochemicals instead, to talk to Martyn Southwick. He seemed a decent guy and he might have some leads.

"Taxi!" It was the ringtone of a young person's mobile. The only thing was that Bluey didn't fit the demographic! He glanced at the screen and it announced "CAITLIN." His heart missed a beat. She was ringing him, so she must be OK. He accepted the call. "Caitlin, thank heavens you're…"

"Shut up!" interrupted the voice. It was mature, male and malevolent. Bluey's heart missed several more beats.

"Nah listen. Yo need to fix it so as the pig don't come up to the surface. Know wa' I mean?"

"What do you expect me to do?"

Simon W. Pain

"Yo's Ashe, ain't yer? Yo can fix it. Ye've got 48 hours, otherwise we'll be sending you the girl back in instalments." The line went dead.

Bluey had to regain his composure for a while before driving on to Duroc. The car park was just inside the main gate. It was just before 8:30 in the morning and obviously people were arriving to start work. As he drove along the lines of cars, he noticed three young people clustered around a white car, obviously admiring it and chatting animatedly. He parked the car, and walked back towards the offices. The three young people were waxing lyrical about the ermine white vehicle with the Sherwood green stripe. It was an elderly but classic, Lotus Cortina. Bluey stopped to talk to them.

"Isn't it a beauty?" said one of the young men.

Bluey agreed. "Do you know who owns it?" They didn't. Apparently, it had not been there before. One of the young men said, "Don't you think it is a bit unusual for a car of that age to have a modern number plate?" Of course, why hadn't Bluey realised? The number on the car was "SF 65 XHZ" and it was mounted on the modern ballotini reflective back plate. It was the car that had been stolen from the old man in Falkirk. But the young man was right—why did a car that must be nearly 50 years old carry a registration plate that was less than 10 years old? The style of number plates had changed in the intervening years, and although it was possible to buy personalised number plates, "SF 65 XHZ" somehow didn't seem like someone's initials. Furthermore, a car of that age wouldn't normally have had a reflective number plate. He went into the office reception, to check in. He explained who he was and at the same time asked the receptionist if they kept a register of cars that were authorised to use the car park. They didn't. She recognised most of the employees' cars. Did he have a particular one in mind? Bluey pointed to the Lotus Cortina. She didn't recognise it, and

Duroc

said that it ought to have been in the visitors' parking area. Bluey suddenly had an overwhelming urge to talk to his friend Sergeant Crieff again. There was something that he wanted to check. So he apologised to the receptionist and headed back to his car.

As usual, Jim Crieff was at his desk. Bluey wanted to know more details about the Lotus Cortina. Jim brought up the details on the DVLA website.

"Well, what do you know, Bluey?" he said. "Your Lotus Cortina is not a Lotus Cortina at all. It's a Volvo!"

"What?" said Bluey.

"Aye, the registration number you gave me is a Volvo. Someone's being a bit naughty and has switched the number plates around." The friendly bobby then asked Bluey to wait for a moment, as there was a note on the file. "Well, what do you know?" he said again. "Do you remember a hit and run a week or two ago, where a radiographer was run off the road? Well, your SF 65 XHZ is the very same Volvo that was involved in that R.T.A. Although the car was burned out, our traffic boys have just spent the week-end tracing engine numbers, and they have come up trumps!"

So, if the registration number fit the Volvo, what was the correct registration number of the Lotus? Also, maybe the old man in Falkirk, who claimed to have had his pride and joy of a Lotus Cortina stolen, wasn't so innocent after all. Someone had to arrange to switch the number plates, and that had to have been done before the radiographer was rendered unfit to travel to the *Merganser*. Even more puzzling was why had the unclaimed Lotus been dumped in the Duroc Petrochemicals car park?

Was this random or another link to Duroc? First he needed to convey the good news to the old petrol head in Falkirk—his dream car had been found. Bluey wondered if the news would be welcome or not.

Twenty minutes later, Bluey pulled up outside the old petrol head's house. The street still looked dismal. He knocked on the door and waited. No answer. The old man must have gone out to drown his sorrows. Bluey tried again, but still no answer. He scribbled a note with his phone number, saying that the car had been found, asking the man to give Bluey a phone call. He put it through the letter box. As he returned to the car and drove away, the curtains of the house twitched again.

Chapter 18

Back on the MS *Merganser*, the welding and testing of pipeline branches had been completed. The team of five men from Scottish Pipeline Services were in the pressure chambers, ready to take the diving bells down to the habitat. The task was to install the large valves onto the branches in readiness for cutting through the pipe walls using an air-driven trepanning cutter. The valves and the trepanning machine had already been lowered to the seabed. The valves were heavy, and although they were special lightweight versions, it was still a challenge for the team, hence the need for five divers, as there was a lot of manhandling involved. Both diving bells were used to ferry the team to the habitat, as in addition to the team members there was also a single bellman. The habitat had been hoisted to one side to allow the large team to lift the valves into place, but that meant working in diving gear in wet conditions. It was always better and safer to work inside the habitat in the dry, but that just wasn't possible. The weight of one of the valves was taken on a hoist and carefully positioned over the branch. Eighteen large bolts were dropped into place around the valve flange and were then tightened. The valve handwheel was operated to ensure that it would open and close. The first valve was successfully installed in less than 20 minutes. The second valve was also fitted very quickly. Stylo gave his team of divers the OK signal. All the other divers responded with an identical gesture, headed back to their respective diving bells and then returned to the hyperbaric chambers on the ship. No more could be done until the next day, when the same team would return to install the large trepanning machine, cut through the branch into the pipeline and then plug the pipe adjacent to where the pig was stuck.

Tomorrow came around soon enough, and the Scottish Pipeline Services team were back on the seabed. The cutting machines were very cumbersome and long, because the cutter had to be designed to retract through the branch and valve before the cutting machine could be removed. It was a potentially risky job, but Stylo's team had done this many times before, although it was always much more difficult underwater. The cutter was bolted to the branch valve, and the machine started to slowly cut its way into the pipe wall. The air motor stopped once the cutter had travelled its required distance and a circular section of pipe called the "coupon" had been cut out. This was the critical bit. The machine was designed to hold the coupon on the end of the cutter whilst the cutter was retracted and the valve closed. If the coupon was dropped into the pipe, not only would they never be able to get it out, but it would be in the way of the plug that they intended to put into the pipe. Dropping the coupon would be a disaster and the USP1 pipeline would be permanently blocked, meaning that the pig would have to stay in the pipe for evermore.

Luckily, they didn't drop the coupon after the first cut.

*****

Caitlin sobbed quietly in the dark. She had lost track of how long she had been in the metal box. It was still pitch dark, and she couldn't even see her own hand. She had been in here for hours, but it was still dark. Surely there must be some daylight soon. In the background she heard some very faint sounds. It

Duroc

sounded like some sort of klaxon or alarm. Maybe a fire alarm sounding. That's all she needed, to be captive inside a metal box when there could be a fire outside. She wondered if anyone would come for her. She realized that only her captors knew where she was. There was little chance of a rescue mission. No one would know where to look for her. Suddenly she heard noises resounding through her box-like prison. A quiet, screeching sound. Suddenly a tunnel of daylight blasted into her prison, as a manhole was thrown open in one of the walls. It was blinding. The joy of light was tempered by the fact that she had been in the dark for so long that her aching eyes couldn't compensate for the sudden brightness. There was a thump as something was throw into her prison space, and then the manhole clanged shut again, followed by the screeching of doing up tamper proof bolts to ensure her confinement. What she did understand now was that, although she hadn't realised it, she had been only three metres away from the manhole. As she brushed the tears away from her eyes, her mind worked fast. What she had seen during the brief flash of dazzling daylight was that she was not in a metal box. Yes, the construction was metal, but she had seen just enough to realise that she was inside some sort of a large tank. There was some good news—the tank appeared to be empty! In fact, she realised that because of the rusty deposits on the floor, it seemed as though it had been empty for some time.

Although the darkness had returned, she decided to try and find whatever had been thrown into the tank. She crawled on all fours in the direction of the manhole, ploughing her way through the rust and filth. She didn't find the box, but she found the manhole. She followed the curving wall of the tank for a few metres, and then turned around and cautiously standing up went back for about six metres before turning round and groping her way back again. Suddenly she tripped over a cardboard box, spilling its contents. It was quite large. The first item she found was an empty bucket. She guessed that that was supposed to be her toilet. She felt around on the floor. It seemed that there were some items of food and a pop bottle. And something else—a small cylindrical object. She ran her hands around the object and got such a start when a dazzling beam of light came on, that she dropped the torch! It was only small, so it wasn't going to last too long. She used the light to gather up her food and a rolled-up sleeping bag into the box and quickly moved it to the side of the tank, so that she could find it again in the dark. The tank walls were curved, like a huge vertical cylinder. If she walked long enough, she should always be able to get back to the food box, but she needed to find out more about her prison whilst her torch still worked.

    She scanned the torch beam like a searchlight around the inside of the tank. It was old and rusty everywhere. It was about 20 metres in diameter, but she couldn't see how far up the roof was. From her abductors' point of view, it was impregnable: there was only one entrance and that was the manhole, which was presumably bolted from the outside. She took some of the bread and hunks of cheese that were in her box. Switching out the light, she munched in the dark. Food gave her inner strength. She wasn't sobbing now, she was scheming! There was about enough food and water to sustain her for somewhere between 12-24 hours. Did that mean that her captors wouldn't be back until this time tomorrow? She used the torch to see her watch. It was 10:32, and she had seen daylight, so it must be morning. But, whatever the time, how could she get out of the tank? She would use the available torchlight to do another survey of her prison. She had to be quick and conserve the torch battery. The tank was old but it was dry, and various bits of steel angle iron and an old nut and bolt were partially hidden in the dust on the floor. She gathered up the scrap items and left

Duroc

then by the box, thinking that they might be needed later. She thought that outside her tank might be somewhere where people worked. Unless all the workers were in league with her captors, she guessed that there might not be a permanent guard on her prison. Her way out had to be to make a noise to attract attention whilst her abductors were away. The problem was that she didn't know all of her captors, or whether they could hear any noises made inside the tank. She was thinking more clearly now. She remembered that when the manhole had been opened to throw the box in, there hadn't been a lot of noise outside. The tank was probably in part of an industrial complex. Industrial workplaces are often quite noisy, but this was not. She guessed that she could be in some remote tank farm, some distance from the factory that it was serving. What she was quite sure of was that the tank was redundant and hadn't been used for a very long time. Perhaps the whole area outside was redundant? Then she remembered the sound of the klaxon. It had sounded like the sort of alarm that is heard regularly on chemical plants. It had been coming from a distance, so she was probably on the site of some sort of chemical plant. She smiled to herself. There was only one land-based chemical plant where people might want to incarcerate her. She was making progress —she thought that she knew where she was. All she needed to do now was to get someone to come and rescue her, and with that thought, she started banging the metal bolt on the wall of the tank. The sound boomed around the storage facility at Duroc Petrochemicals. But the plant had re-established feedstock and was noisily coming back on line and so no one heard.

*****

Stylo and his team were returning once again in the Liberty diving bell to complete the second tapping operation into the pipeline. The branch that they were working on was on the upstream side of the pig, nearest to the Gannet Gamma rig. As before, the task had to be to remove the coupon in the top side of the pipe, without dropping it inside the pipe. Only this time they weren't so lucky. Or maybe they were. Moura had instructed Stylo to make sure that, whatever happened, the pig was not recovered. What better way than to permanently block the pipe with a dropped coupon? It wouldn't do Scottish Pipeline Services' reputation much good, but the GG were holding them responsible anyway, as it was their pig that had got stuck. If the coupon was dropped, they couldn't put a stopper in the pipe, and either the USP1 pipeline would have to be abandoned, or they would have to install yet another branch and a much longer by-pass. That would take a long time.

The fact that the second coupon was dropped was communicated to the *Merganser*. The air in the dive control room went blue for a considerable time, because everyone understood what that meant. Stylo suggested that before they returned to the ship they install the stopper in the downstream branch, but this was not approved by the GG installation manager. He wanted to see if he could transfer any feedstock through to the on-shore plant, which had been waiting to start up for two weeks now. The team returned to the pressure chambers on the ship four hours later to face an inquest into what had gone wrong. It would take another two weeks for a new branch to be welded onto the pipeline, and for the by-pass to be finally built.

Extraordinarily, the feedstock tank at Duroc Petrochemicals started to refill. No one seemed to question it—they were only too pleased to be able to re-start the plant and become a cash generator again.

The Duroc Petrochemicals fitter, Jim Cleary, and his wayward young apprentice Dougie Watson were still working in the storage area. Things had been very quiet for a few days whilst

Duroc

the plant had been unable to get feedstock, but now it was all systems go, and they were starting up the main plant again. Jim liked to encourage Dougie to use his initiative. Today Jim was maintaining a pump, whilst Dougie was carrying out routine inspections and lubrication. It was another dull day for Dougie. The storage compound was at the perimeter of the site and at least half a mile from the main production plant. During the start-up of the plant, there were regular klaxon alarms sounding as the operators trimmed the plant to give steady production, but Dougie ignored them. He trudged around the tanks, checking for anything abnormal. Several of the tanks were redundant and out of use, so there was no point in going over to them. As he rounded the base of a small green tank, he noticed tyre tracks in the mud, leading to a locked gate in the perimeter fence. He was curious, and bent down. The tracks seemed fresh. Closer examination of the gate showed that the locking chain had been cut. He followed the car tracks. They were leading to one of the large redundant tanks. They went right up to the manhole cover in the side of the tank. The tank was very rusty, but there was evidence that someone had been tampering with the manhole bolts. They were well oiled, and instead of 36 bolts, there were only four but unusually they were non-standard tamperproof bolts, with one of those four having a padlock on each end. He noticed a sheet of corrugated iron on the floor near the tank manhole. Why was that there? He idly tapped his spanner on the manhole door whilst he thought. Suddenly from inside the tank there was a metallic knocking noise.

Dougie froze. He called to Jim and told him to hurry. The elderly fitter bumbled his way across, slightly irritated at being called by his protégé.

Dougie tapped the manhole again. There was an immediate metallic response. "There's someone in there!" Jim cried. "Yes, but we can't unbolt the manhole. Someone has changed the bolts to anti-tamper fittings. My spanners won't undo those. It needs a special key." Said Dougie, and he immediately started climbing the external staircase on the tank wall to get up to the roof. When he reached the roof he walked to the apex—and Caitlin heard every footstep.

On top of the roof was a large, hinged emergency vent which Dougie swung open. He stared down into the tank. It was pitch black in there. He couldn't see a thing. "Is anyone there?"

A rather feeble female voice answered, "Help me!"

Bloody hell, there is someone in there, thought Dougie. By this time, Jim Cleary had staggered to the top of the staircase. The two tradesmen knelt on the roof and shone the torch into the black depths of the tank. The beam cast around the area, but initially they could see nothing.

"There!" said Jim. The torchlight had picked out a human form crumpled on the tank floor. They called to the figure to see if it responded. Caitlin called out her name and managed to add that she didn't know how long she'd been incarcerated. Jim said he would get help.

Caitlin panicked. "No! I don't know who the people are or what they are wanting to do. There could be others. Am I at Duroc?" Jim said she was in the Duroc Petrochemicals storage compound. Caitlin told them not to mention this to anyone, but to contact Bluey Scrimshaw at Ashe. He would then come and find her. There were malicious goings on at Duroc, and she couldn't trust anyone.

So why would she trust these two?

Dougie and Jim almost fell down the tank staircase in their haste as they rushed to get help.

*****

Bluey drove straight home after his fruitless visit to the petrol head's house. It was late afternoon and starting to turn

Duroc

dusky. Debbie was still a bit frosty about the fact that he hadn't taken the boys to football at the week-end. As he came in the door, he smiled to break the ice, but Debbie was not ready for forgiveness yet. His phone rang. Not great timing. He apologised to his wife and took the call. It was some fitter from Duroc talking very quietly and asking if he knew someone called Caitlin. Of course he did.

The fitter said he knew where she was. But it was dangerous for him to speak. Could he meet Bluey tonight at midnight at the north emergency gate in the Duroc Petrochemicals perimeter fence? The man said his name was Jim Cleary. He told Bluey to wear something dark and bring a powerful torch, a monkey wrench and a 30-metre rope. The call ended there, with many more questions than answers.

Debbie was glowering. He would have to tell her about Caitlin, as he would have to go out again tonight to find her. Debbie melted at his story. He explained that it had been too dangerous to tell her what was going on. She flung her arms around him, kissing his face as if she were a teenager. But it *would* be dangerous, and he swore her to secrecy. Bluey told her that if anything went wrong—if he didn't get back by dawn —she must call the police, and they would need to search Duroc Petrochemicals storage compound. He thought that was where he would find Caitlin.

Bluey gathered a few essential items from his garage and then drove to the Duroc plant. He parked his car about a quarter of a mile from the emergency gate and, shouldering the pack of equipment from his garage, he walked the last section of the fence to the gate, arriving exactly at midnight. The lights from the Duroc plant did little to improve visibility at the storage area, which was basically pitch dark. He waited patiently at the gate, looking furtively over his shoulder to see if he was being watched. A few minutes later he saw two figures in dark overalls and hard hats moving swiftly towards him. He hesitated; he hadn't expected two. Not only that, but he didn't even know what this fitter, called Jim Cleary, looked like. It could be anyone. It could be Caitlin's captors. He suddenly realised how vulnerable he was. No one other than Debbie knew where he was going, and the opposition were ruthless.

"Are you Bluey?" came the call across the darkness.

Did he admit it? He was in deep and had to trust someone. "Yes."

The emergency gate swung open. In the dark, Bluey faced a rather ponderous but short middle-aged man. He introduced himself as Jim. His colleague was a young man who was clearly wired by the events of the night. Jim introduced Dougie as his apprentice. He said he'd thought that they might need some youthful energy. For Dougie it was by far the best thing that had happened in his apprenticeship so far. It even topped riding his Kawasaki!

"Right let's get in that manhole" said Bluey

"Can't—It's locked with tamper proof bolts and we've got no key" said Jim. "We need to go in via the emergency vent hatch".

Bluey nodded, and without further discussion they started to climb the staircase up to the tank roof. Caitlin, wide-eyed, heard the footsteps climbing the stairs wrapped around the outside of the tank. There were several people going up to the roof. The footsteps echoed across the roof. Who were they? Suddenly the emergency vent was thrown open and a shaft of moonlight shone down, but its intensity was not enough to illuminate the inside of the tank. She saw three heads peering in through the open vent.

"Caitlin—*Caitlin—Caitlin—Caitlin*..." Bluey had completely misjudged how loudly he called, and her name resonated in echoes through the tank and out into the open air. The three

Duroc

rescuers flattened themselves to the roof, looking around anxiously to see if anyone else had heard. Nothing stirred.

"Bluey, is that you?—*Bluey, is that you?—Bluey, is that you?...*" Caitlin had whispered, thinking it was too risky to reply. But there was still an echo.

They were going in. Bluey suddenly realised why Dougie the apprentice was there. It seemed he was a bit of a climber in his spare time. Without a sound, Dougie took the rope from Bluey's pack, anchored one end to the base of the handrail around the top of the tank, took a descendeur out of his overalls pocket and, without a word, started to lower himself into the large, open vent hatchway. As soon as he was inside the roof, Bluey saw him expertly abseil down the rope in a smooth and silent glide. He was impressed.

Caitlin looked up just in time to see a James Bond-style figure hurtling towards her. He was completely silent. Just before he would have smashed into the floor, Dougie pulled down on the descendeur and his ride came to a gentle stop, with his feet firmly on the floor. Caitlin beamed at her hero. He put his finger to his lips to indicate no more echoes. He took out a pencil torch and started to check her over. She looked as though she had done 10 rounds in a mud wrestling match, and she'd lost her trousers, too. Even in that state, Dougie could tell she was a looker—he bet she brushed up well.

There hadn't been much time to discuss the details of getting Caitlin out, but Dougie knew that there were tamper proof bolts on the main manhole entrance, and so the only way out was the way he had come in. He eyed Caitlin's rusty figure carefully and estimated that she probably didn't weigh much more than 120pounds. Two big guys on the roof should be able to pull her up. Putting his fingers to his lips again, he expertly removed the rope end from himself and tried a tight bowline around her waist, indicating silently that she should hold onto the rope. He gave a tug on the rope and with a slight shriek she swung into the air.

On top of the roof, Bluey and Jim were pulling with all their might. It was easier to pull when standing up, but, as they did so, Jim placed a hand on Bluey's arm to signal him to stop. Headlights were bouncing along the rough road that led to the emergency gate. They would be silhouetted against the lights of the plant in the background. As a duo, they flattened themselves against the roof, and Caitlin's progress towards freedom came to a sudden halt. Bluey hoped that she wouldn't call out. The car came to a stop outside the fence and the lights went out. A single shadowy figure got out and went around to the boot. A large boot lid opened. Bluey thought it looked familiar. The shadowy figure took out a box of some sort, and slammed the lid with a little too much enthusiasm and far too much noise. The figure headed to the gate and across to the tank manhole. The figure stopped and took a tool out of the box and started to undo the four remaining tamper proof bolts in the manhole cover. The quiet squeal of the turning nuts was amplified within the tank. Dougie knew immediately what was happening; he heard that sound every day in his work. He looked up. Caitlin was dangling bare-legged in mid-air and she wasn't moving upwards. He didn't know why the lifting had stopped. Caitlin had let go with one hand and was pointing towards the manhole. He moved silently there and stubbed his toe on a heavy piece of angle iron. He realised she was indicating that as a weapon. The noises at the manhole had almost stopped now. Just a couple of clicks as the padlocks were removed. There was a metallic sound as the manhole swung open and the box was tossed inside the tank. The manhole was a circle 20 inches in diameter, and so to get in the figure came through feet first with a large torch blazing. Dougie flattened himself against the walls, absolutely silent. The shadowy figure stood up, picked up

Duroc

the box and scanned around the tank, looking for his hostage. She didn't seem to be there. He shone the beam up into the upper space and it picked out Caitlin's bare legs. The mouth in his unshaven face opened in astonishment. "What the... Ooooff!" Dougie had swung the heavy piece of angle iron, catching him smack in the centre of the box he was holding to his chest. The box exploded into pieces as the Unshaven One was sent spinning onto the dusty floor, clutching two broken ribs.

Dougie called to Bluey to haul Caitlin up and quickly took a mobile phone photo of Caitlin's kidnapper. He ran to the manhole, sprang through it like an experienced fitter and slammed the cover shut. There was a sound of squeaking as he quickly screwed the nuts back in place to lock the kidnapper into his own prison. Served him right.

As Dougie turned around, he met Jim and Bluey supporting a weakened Caitlin down the last few stairs from the roof. They headed towards the emergency gate. As they approached the kidnapper's car, Bluey told Dougie to get a photo, but just as the camera phone flashed, revealing a classic white car with green stripes, the car lights came on, the engine roared into life and the car reversed away at a frightening speed. It was another ten minutes before the intrepid four arrived at Bluey's car. Bluey was pretty sure that it wouldn't be long before Moura knew about Caitlin's escape and would be planning revenge. However, he had two urgent tasks: to get Caitlin back home, or at least into a safe place, and to notify his police chum about the man they had left behind in the tank. Judging by what Dougie said, he would be in need of fairly urgent medical attention! For Dougie it had been a good night to be an apprentice fitter, although Bluey was a bit concerned when he looked in his rearview mirror and saw Caitlin snuggled up to her hero, the young man on the back seat!

Chapter 19

Moura was absolutely beside himself. He had just heard that the hostage had flown. They had told him that she would never be found in the redundant tank. Nobody ever went there. His bargaining chip had evaporated. Moura suspected that someone who worked in the Duroc Petrochemicals storage compound had found out. There weren't many people working there. He could discover who it might be. It looked as though the escape had been organised by Ashe. What made things even worse was that two of his key people had been picked up by the police in the early hours of the morning. One had been found locked inside the tank, with two broken ribs. He was under police guard in hospital and was about to be charged with kidnapping. A second man had also been picked up based on Bluey's information. He was an old petrol head who owned a classic Lotus Cortina with a faulty number plate, who would also have some serious explaining to do about a Volvo road traffic accident two weeks earlier.

Moura was not happy when he got annoying phone calls in the middle of the night. This wasn't the first time that his people had turned out to be a load of incompetents, but of course he'd chosen them! He called the man he knew he could rely on. Stylo answered. He said little but just nodded and grunted understanding. Things were going wrong. He had always expected it, and he had anticipated the need for the next "ratchet up" in

Duroc

terms of their action. It was convenient that Stylo was still billeted on the MS *Merganser*, waiting to finish the delayed pipeline stoppling.

*****

    The *Merganser* had been on station above the stuck pig now for four weeks. After the fiasco of dropping the coupon into the pipe at the upstream branch, a lot of additional work had been required to avoid abandoning the USP1 pipeline. Another branch had to be acquired and delivered to the *Merganser* and then welded to the pipeline, along with additional lengths of by-pass pipe, as the by-pass was now longer than originally planned. The new branch had been welded, tested and had the valve fitted. Stylo and his team from Scottish Pipeline Services had been told personally by the GG installation manager that if they messed up the cutting of the coupon from the pipeline this time, they would never ever work again in the North Sea. And he meant it. Stylo was not one of the incompetent ones, and this coupon was cut out and removed without any calamity.

    The next job was also for the Scottish Pipeline team, because no one else had the equipment or skill to do it. They needed to install the stopples through the two outer branches. The stopples were steel discs slightly smaller than the inside of the pipe which were surrounded by rubber seals designed to resist the corrosive effects of the pipeline contents. They were mounted on a weird, rather ridiculous contraption made of rods and cranks. Placing the stopple inside the branch and through the hole in the pipe wall, it was possible, by skilfully manipulating the rods and cranks, to turn the stopple through the 90-degree turn and insert it permanently around the corner. The stopples were placed on the side of the branch nearest to the stuck pig, one in front and one behind. The installation of the stopples went perfectly. Stylo didn't dare mess the procedure up this time, as he had future plans.

Simon W. Pain

The Scottish Pipeline Services team had finished their contract. The team could return to base, but Stylo needed to stay to recover the pig. In the meantime, the *Merganser*'s welders returned to the depths to connect up the by-pass pipework. And now, four weeks after the pig had got stuck, the bypass pipe was not only ready, but was in commission. Full flows had been re-established in the pipeline. All that needed to happen now was that the old section of pipeline that housed the stuck pig between the two isolations had to be cut out so that a new section (without a pig stuck in it) could be welded in. Then the stopples could be removed, the original flow direction would be back to normal, and the MS *Merganser* could leave and sort out someone else's problems!

The cutting of the pipe section containing the stuck pig was to be done by a team of four divers. Three of the men were regulars from the *Merganser* dive teams, and Stylo had arranged to be there because it was his pig. Moura wanted the pig to be left on the sea-bed. They could always return for it later, but Ashe had decreed that the cause of the sticking must be established, and so the pig had to come up onto the deck of the *Merganser*.

The four divers were going through pressurisation. Two divers, Terry and Hamish, were in one chamber, and Stylo and the bellman were in the second chamber. Stylo wasn't needed for the cutting work. Two divers plus the bellman could handle that easily. Working inside the habitat, they used a small hydraulically powered rotary cutter attached to a band, which kept the cutter in contact with the pipe until each 360-degree cut was finished. The two pipe cuts were made either side of the location where the radiographers had located the pig and took no more than three hours. The welders returned to the Big Ben diving bell and then went back to the decompression chamber on board ship. Their saturation diving spell was not yet completed, as they would have to return to put a new piece of pipe in place of the section that they had just cut out. So the two divers doing the cutting returned to the first hyperbaric chamber and the bellman joined Stylo in the second chamber. After a basic evening meal and some TV and rather dodgy internet searches, the four men hit their bunks and slept soundly.

Elsewhere, things were not going so well. A gloved hand was on the decompression valve for the first chamber. The pressure suddenly started to drop. But the decompression was not noticed by the dive control room operator. The pressure was dropping far too quickly. Terry was the first to waken. He felt really groggy. Unknown to him, nitrogen gas bubbles were starting to build up at his elbows and knees. Initially he had feelings of numbness, and then the pain hit him. He yelled out in agony, waking Hamish. His muscles were degassing faster than if he had just risen to the water surface. Hamish also felt muddled. He looked across at Terry, who was doubled up on his side on his bunk. He realised that Terry was getting "the bends." His own torment was starting now. They must be decompressing. He needed to alert dive control. Hamish called out, but there was no response from the control room. He felt pains in his back. The quiet of the chamber was interrupted by Terry's moaning and a ringing in his own ears. The pains were starting in his elbows. He needed to get help. He fell out of his bunk and tried to reach the intercom button. It was purgatory. He reached the intercom, but there was no response. The lines were dead. He needed to reach the emergency button to summon help. Everything in the chamber looked normal, except for the fact that its two occupants were writhing in agony. Now Hamish's legs were not in so much pain, they were becoming numb. Moving was difficult. A creeping paralysis was spreading up towards his waist, but his attention was pre-occupied with the crippling pain in his elbows. He doubled up on the floor.

Simon W. Pain

Terry was quiet now. Was he already in a coma? At least that would give him some relief from the pain. Hamish couldn't reach the big red emergency button. It was too high up the wall. He couldn't think straight. Maybe he could open the hatch and get across to the other chamber? But perhaps Stylo and the bellman were having the same problems. In any case, the hatch wouldn't open unless the air pressure on both sides was equal. He suspected it wasn't. A fog spread across Hamish's mind. He slid slowly down the wall into a foetal position on the floor. Slowly the pain subsided as he sank into a deep coma and total silence. In chamber two, Stylo and the bellman were sleeping soundly. They weren't having the same problems at all!

It was 4 a.m. before dive control realised that Terry and Hamish were not just asleep. Attempts to contact them were in vain. The dive supervisor was called and he identified that the pressure in chamber one was almost back to atmospheric. The chamber had decompressed and no one had noticed. There was no time for recriminations at the moment. That would come later. The urgent action was to start hyperbaric oxygen treatment without delay. This involved 100% oxygen and increasing the pressure again. It was high risk in an environment where there was electricity present, as the whole lot could ignite, so all the power had to be shut off.

*****

Bluey took the call at home. He was thinking and twirling his new Rubik's cube. There had been yet another dangerous incident in the North Sea. This one had again been on the diving support vessel MS *Merganser*. Two saturation divers had been subjected to rapid decompression during the night. Both were in a very bad way with "the bends" and were apparently undergoing recompression treatment at that very moment. He called the *Merganser* on the ship-to-shore link. Apparently the condition of the two divers was touch and go and paramedics were flying out to the ship as they spoke. He had been about to head into work in Falkirk, but changed his plans and arranged to pick up the first chopper out from Dyce. By the time Bluey had landed on the *Merganser*'s heli-deck, it was already too late for Terry. He hadn't made it, and Hamish was still in a bad way inside the compression chamber. The ship's own investigation had started and had immediately replaced the dive control operator. He was undergoing some sort of interrogation by crew members at the moment, and was to be returned to the shore on the chopper that Bluey had arrived on. It didn't take Bluey long to identify the fact that the low-pressure alarms on the chamber were not functioning. In his opinion, it was inevitable that if the alarms were not working, eventually an uncontrolled decompression could and would occur. Although it was too late, there was a hive of activity to find out why the decompression had happened. The maintenance technicians had found that the manual valves controlling the pressure in the chamber had been tampered with, resulting in the pressure in the chamber being vented to the atmosphere. It was clear that the chamber had been sabotaged. Bluey thought to himself that this was not just sabotage. It was murder.

    He obtained a full inventory of the crew and contractors on board and insisted to Findlay Innes, the master of the *Merganser*, that no one should leave the ship until his investigation was completed. After a long series of interviews that were carried out under caution, Bluey responded to a request from Findlay for a meeting. Bluey headed up to the bridge. The master explained that the ship had been in this location for over four weeks and was running low on fuel and supplies. The task of removing the stuck pig was almost complete. The pipeline was cut, and so all that needed to happen now was that the old section of pipe containing the pig needed to be raised to the surface and a new section of pipe welded in place. If the chamber pressure alarm systems were sorted out and tested, and the pressure venting systems were made tamper-proof by locks, could they continue to dive? They felt that it would only take two more days of underwater work to complete the job, and then they could be away and back to port. Port would definitely be the safest place to be, much safer than staying at sea, especially as it was predicted that the weather would change.

Bluey carefully recounted all the steps that he required them to take before permitting dives to resume. In particular, he had found that the communication wires had been disconnected in chamber one, where the decompression had occurred. This confirmed that the decompression had been intentional. The plan was to use the two divers who were in chamber 2 and still under saturation conditions to go down and retrieve the section of cut pipe containing the stuck pig. One of these divers was the Scottish Pipeline Services contractor Stylo.

It took 48 hours before Bluey was satisfied that the new alarms, controls and communications links were not only in place but fully tested and working. He then gave permission for diving to recommence. Stylo and his bellman took the Liberty diving bell taxi service down to the seabed. All the activity was being closely monitored by a crowd of people in the dive control room, including the dive supervisor, the operator and Bluey. As Stylo carefully made his way from the Liberty bell to where the pipe had been cut, the team in the control room anxiously watched his progress as it was beamed up to the TV monitors from his helmet camera. It was like watching a slow-motion picture. There on the screen in the greenish light of the camera was the section of cut pipe. It was about three metres in length and was lying on the seabed. Stylo's job was to prepare it for lifting by placing strops around the pipe to get a level lift. They didn't want the pig to fall out of the pipe as it was being lifted

Duroc

back up to the ship. Bluey watched the screen as Stylo slowly threaded one of the strops through the pipe and connected it to the hoist wire that had been lowered from the deck of the *Merganser*.

"How can he do that?" Bluey asked the dive supervisor.

"What?"

"How can he thread the lifting strop through the pipe? Surely, the pig should be in the way?"

It suddenly dawned on the dive supervisor what Bluey meant. He turned to the operator and told him to instruct the diver to stop and shine his camera up the cut pipe. For a moment, turbid particles obscured the video picture as Stylo moved. Then very slowly, as the cloudiness cleared, an image of the cut pipe came into view. Stylo's helmet camera was looking straight down the inside of the cut pipe. The lights shone straight through the empty pipe. There was a gasp in the dive control room. The pig had disappeared!

Chapter 20

It was a typical Scottish afternoon. There was no need for a weather forecast: as usual, the weather was either "raining" or the only other alternative, "just about to rain". Caitlin was in the office staring ponderously out of the window, reflecting on the events of the last few days. It wasn't every day that you set out to get some much-needed exercise and ended up locked inside a chemical tank. But the tables had been turned, and her evil-looking, unshaven captor had himself been trapped in the tank and was now awaiting His Majesty's pleasure. That was all down to the heroics of a young Duroc apprentice fitter by the name of Dougie Watson. She had been impressed by Dougie's abseiling into the tank to come to her rescue. In fact, she had been so impressed that she had already met up with him twice in the last three days. Once to say "thank you." And the second time had been more of an assignation. She liked Dougie, and he seemed to like her. That was an understatement for Dougie. When they had rescued Caitlin, she had looked as though she had just been through a tornado, but when she came to see him a day later, he realized he'd been right -- she did scrub up well!" It was one of those life-changing moments. The priorities in Dougie's life had suddenly changed. Football was kicked into touch, the Kawasaki KX450-SR was suddenly just a means of transport, and girls were no longer his second priority, they

Duroc

were top of the list. To be more precise, one girl in particular, and her name was Caitlin.

The phone was ringing. All the health and safety inspectors were out of the office. Caitlin sauntered over to her desk and picked up the handset. "Alba Safety and Health Executive, Caitlin Barland speaking. How can I help?"

"Caitlin, its Dougie Watson at Duroc Petrochemicals." Her heart leapt.

"I think you should get over here to the Duroc plant straight away. There's something that you may want to see!" gasped Dougie.

"What is it, Dougie?"

"Don't talk to anyone on the way in. I'll meet you at the office's reception desk and we'll go straight to the storage compound."

Caitlin was intrigued. She wasted no time in heading up to Duroc on her trusty Triumph. Sure enough, Dougie was there. Without thinking, she gave him a kiss on the cheek. Dougie beamed. It was just great being a fourth-year apprentice! He reciprocated and was almost swamped by her heady perfume. The middle-aged receptionist silently gave a disapproving look as Dougie checked Caitlin in.

Without a word to clarify where they were going, Dougie led Caitlin out of the office building and walked for about 600 yards around the perimeter of the plant, heading towards a large tank farm.

Dougie nodded towards one of the large but rather rusty-looking tanks. "Looks better from the outside, doesn't it?" She suddenly realised that they were looking at her former prison. In daylight somehow it didn't seem so threatening, but she didn't want to linger. Dougie strode on and then came to an abrupt stop. "Look at that," he said.

Caitlin looked at a strange array of pipework to her left.

"It's a pig trap," said Dougie, adding the word "apparently." "But just look at the indicator."

Caitlin looked towards the top of the light green horizontal pipework. On top of the large pipe there was a small device that was indicating that there was a pig in the trap.

"So what?" she said.

"There wasn't one there yesterday, and we've had no notification that a pig has been launched, other than the one stuck in USP1."

Caitlin immediately realised the enormity of the situation. She needed to speak to Bluey straight away. Since the storage area was full of flammable materials, she knew she couldn't use her mobile phone here, and so she asked Dougie to stay by the pig trap and ensure that no one tried to remove the pig from the trap. If anyone queried it, then it was an order from Ashe. Meanwhile she went straight back to the offices to find a private room from which to call Bluey.

Bluey was still out on the MS *Merganser*. He answered Caitlin's phone call and briefly told her about the diver decompressions. Sadly, there had been one fatality and one other victim who was now on his way to the Aberdeen Royal Infirmary. He was not at all sure that the second victim would survive. Bluey was now even more convinced that this was a case of murder. He went on to recall how the stuck pig had mysteriously disappeared.

At that point Caitlin interrupted and told him that that was the reason she was calling. She thought she might know where the pig was. She said that the apprentice, Dougie Watson, had discovered an unexpected arrival in one of the pig traps at Duroc Petrochemicals. The pig was still in the trap, and she didn't think anyone else knew about it yet. She thought it might be the missing pig from USP1, although why it should have suddenly become unstuck, she couldn't guess. Bluey speculated

Duroc

that perhaps the vibrations caused when Scottish Pipeline Services were cutting their way through the newly welded branches had been sufficient to release the pig. But how it had happened seemed academic at this point—the urgent need was to get the pig out of the trap and find out if it contained something illegal. There had been several attempts to disrupt or prevent the removal of the pig, and so Bluey thought that they should anticipate another effort to purloin the pig. Since Bluey was stuck out on the *Merganser*, he told Caitlin to get an immediate prohibition order from their boss at Ashe, to prevent anyone other than Ashe removing the pig. Bluey said he would contact the office, if Caitlin would hand the prohibition order over to the plant manager, Brodric Reynolds, in person. Caitlin asked how she should stop someone who was determined to unload the pig. It was clear she would need help. Bluey gave her the name of detective Jim Crieff at the Scottish Police Service and suggested that the boys in blue should be asked to mount a guard. He would get the next chopper home in the morning.

*****

It was 11 o'clock on Wednesday morning. Bluey had just flown back into Dyce and had gone straight to the Duroc Petrochemicals plant without even stopping to go home. There was quite a crowd milling around the pig trap when Bluey arrived. Caitlin was there with Martyn Southwick, the Duroc Petrochemicals health and safety adviser. There were two tired-looking police constables who had been there all night, and Dougie Watson and his mentor Jim Cleary were there to actually do the work! A wagon driver with a small pick-up truck was also on hand so that the pig could be taken directly to the safekeeping of Ashe's laboratory in Falkirk.

Simon W. Pain

The physical removal of the pig was quite straightforward. The trap was designed with quick-release mechanisms and lifting beams to allow the pig to be handled easily. The trap was opened and Jim and Dougie pulled it onto the lifting beam and from there onto the back of the pick-up truck. In less than 15 minutes, the pig had been retrieved and was ready for despatch to the laboratory in Falkirk. As Caitlin passed Jim Cleary, he turned and said, "I don't know what you've done to Dougie, lassie, but I've never seen him so keen and motivated!" Caitlin just smiled.

Suddenly Martyn Southwick said to Bluey, "We should stop. I think that pig has a radio-active tracer on it!"

Of course! Bluey had forgotten about the tracer. They all pulled back and summoned urgent help from Industrial Radiography Ltd to safely remove the tracer. This time IRL sent their two best operatives, and there were no last-minute substitutions. The tracer was successfully removed before lunchtime.

They lost no time in inspecting the pig. It was immediately obvious that it had been modified significantly. Bluey took a series of photographs of the outside of the pig. He was no pigging expert, but this did not look conventional. The cups at either end that were used to propel the pig or plough out the rubbish were standard enough, but in between them there was a large container of some sort, with various bolted covers. They used an overhead suspended scale to get the weight of the pig, and then it was placed on the floor on a large piece of clean polythene sheet, in case anything fell out once they started to open it up. It was Caitlin's job to video record the process of opening up the container on the pig. The first task was to clean the oil and grease off it. Once that was done the access cover bolts looked quite new and easy to undo. Clearly the bolts had been replaced recently and had been wired together to prevent them coming loose whilst the pig was moving. Bluey worked first on the cover that was on top of the container in the centre of the pig. He was wearing a Tyvek suit, gloves and a dust mask, not only to protect himself from whatever was in the pig container, but also because he needed to be sure that he followed forensic protocols and did not contaminate the contents, which might form part of the evidence in any future prosecution.

As he lifted the first cover Caitlin could see that the inside did not contain the fancy electronic circuit boards that would normally have been expected, but that it was full of tightly packed packets of some substance. Initially the transparent packs seemed to contain an off-white powder. The way that the powder was packaged immediately suggested drugs to both Bluey and Caitlin. The packets were carefully transferred to a series of clean, empty plastic boxes. As they handled the packets, it became clear that they were not all the same. And they didn't actually contain powder, but a crystalline substance. In addition, the colours of the crystals varied from off-white to yellow to brown. Neither of the investigators recognised the substance. Bluey called in their drugs expert. He was equally baffled. He had never seen this substance before. However, the way in which it had been packed and the quantity did suggest that it was some form of street drug. It was decided that as the materials were unknown and there was a possibility that they might be used as evidence, one of the packs should be sent to the Scottish Government Forensic Science laboratory for analysis and identification. The remainder of the packages would remain either in the pig or in the plastic box. The room in which the materials were stored was then secured and access was limited to only those who had Bluey's written permission.

It didn't take the Forensic Science lab long to get back to them. A Dr Mark Spencer called the following day. They needed to do further tests, but he was pretty sure that the crystals were a drug called Monkeydust. It was a naturally occurring stimulant drug found in the plant Khat, which is mainly grown in the Yemen. He said that it was known to cause mild euphoria, that can make users feel anxious or paranoid, although it had also been known to produce manic behaviour or hyperactivity. It was also called Butylene M1, or Magic Crystals, although its chemical name was cathinone. He said that in Scotland it was classified as a Class B drug, although in some countries it was being upgraded to Class A. It was available on the internet and marketed as plant food or bath salts. Mark finished his report by saying that typically it was available to street users at £2 per hit.

Bluey and Caitlin were back in Ashe's Falkirk office. As usual, Bluey was idly fiddling with his latest Rubik's cube. He would have to stop losing them. "Don't you think it's a bit odd," mused Bluey, "that the pig is carrying a large quantity of a Class B drug?"

"And Monkeydust is not particularly strong. Its street value is actually quite low," said Caitlin.

"I reckon that the pig held no more than 25 kilos of drugs—so its street value is probably less than £100,000. Don't forget that the street dealer will take a big cut of the profits, so Moura probably only gets perhaps half that, and he will have to buy it in the first place. It seems a lot of hassle to go through to make a fairly modest profit, especially when you see the risks that they are running, don't you think?"

Caitlin agreed. Why would anyone go to all that trouble? It hardly seemed worth the risk. "What if Monkeydust is a loss-leader?" said Caitlin, thinking of how buying milk gets shoppers into the supermarket. "Maybe they want to distract our attention from something else!"

Bluey flicked a full side of reds on his Rubik's cube. "Maybe. What if it is not a loss-leader? What if the pig is purely a business opportunity for transportation of illicit materials. What if

Duroc

Moura is not in the drugs business at all, but he will transport anything for anyone, if the price is right?"

There were just so many unknowns. They knew the name of Mr Big, but it was just an alias, so they couldn't find him. They knew what the pig had been transporting on this occasion, but was that the real motivation? Bluey and Caitlin decided to take a weekend off whilst they thought about what was going on.

Bluey decided that it was time to call a feedback meeting, to bring the Duroc people up to date on Alba's findings regarding the various recent incidents. He called Brodric Reynolds and asked him to arrange a meeting room, and to ensure that the relevant people from the GG were also present. Reynolds agreed with all the good grace of Ebenezer Scrooge. The meeting was called for the following Thursday in the Duroc Petrochemicals conference room.

Chapter 21

"Oh, what a tangled web we weave!" Bluey said to himself. He stood up and addressed the meeting. "Let me just remind you of what has happened in the last two months." He paused as he cast his eye around the conference room. Twenty pairs of apparently innocent eyes stared back. "There have been 10 incidents during the last two months. The tragedy of those incidents is that nine people have lost their lives, and another nine have ended up having hospital treatment. The common factor between all those incidents is that they were linked in some way or other to your group of companies—the Duroc Group."

"The helicopter crash wasn't linked to Duroc," said Iain, the Duroc Petrochemicals engineer.

"Well, that is a matter of opinion. It was on a flight to the Gannet Gamma, which is owned and operated by Duroc Offshore. It was not only carrying your employees. I would remind you that I was also on that flight. We know that the cause of the helicopter pilot's initial loss of control was that it flew too close to the Duroc Offshore flare stack at a time when there was a sudden very large flare discharge."

"That's not Duroc's fault!" came the irritated response from Jason Suínos, the rig IM.

"We'll see about that. Whatever you think, the relatives of the four Duroc employees who died when the lifeboat went down will take the view that their loved ones were just trying to help their colleagues. However, the helicopter crash is not the main reason why I am here today. I would like to share with you our findings on what else has been going on in relation to the other Duroc incidents." Bluey paused to take a sip of coffee. "Duroc Petrochemicals has been recently acquired at considerable expense. And we know from production control that you were having problems with your feedstock." He turned to Brodric Reynolds. "Why were you short of feedstock?"

"We weren't short of feedstock," replied the combative Reynolds. "We had a short-term cash flow issue."

"And that meant that you couldn't pay for the feedstock?"

"It meant a temporary delay in our payments."

Bluey smiled. "And this temporary delay in paying your bills, did it cause the plant to cease operations?"

"No!" Brodric exclaimed. "The plant shut down because of a boiler feedwater pump failure."

"And what was the cause of that pump failure?" Bluey looked across at Iain, inviting him to comment.

"We found that there was water in the gearbox oil," Iain said.

"Was that water put in the oil sump intentionally?" asked Bluey.

"There is no other reason why water should get inside an otherwise sealed gearbox," Iain answered.

"So, it was sabotaged?"

"Yes, I would say so."

Reynolds glowered across at his engineer.

Bluey turned his attention back to Brodric Reynolds. "This production outage that was caused by the pump gearbox failure would have been expensive. What was the cost to Duroc?"

"Remember it happened when we were short of feedstock, so the cost was minimal."

"Perhaps, but what was the cost? How many thousands of pounds?"

Reynolds paused before he quietly replied, "It cost over 170,000 pounds."

"That's a lot of money!" said Bluey. "Presumably you carry insurance cover for such an event?"

"Yes, but we haven't had our claim settled yet."

"Why?"

"Our insurers, Industrial Protection, are disputing our current claims."

"Claims? Is there more than one?" asked Bluey innocently, already knowing the answer.

"We have also submitted a claim for the bellows failure."

"For how much?"

"One hundred thousand pounds."

"And why are Industrial Protection disputing the claims?"

Brodric hung his head and then said very quietly, "They seem to suspect fraud."

There was a slight intake of breath from some of the more junior staff members at the meeting. Their boss seemed to be almost admitting fraudulent dealings. Bluey had had his first success: Reynolds had confirmed his suspicion that the bellows failure had arisen from a financial scam. The delay caused whilst the bellows was inspected had clearly been intended to allow Duroc to make a further false insurance claim. Industrial Protection would be able to confirm that.

Caitlin was impressed with Bluey; they had always thought that the bellows incident was to do with the business problems that Duroc Petrochemicals were facing. What she was less sure about was how that linked to all the other incidents and the drugs running.

Bluey decided not to pursue Brodric any further at this stage and moved on to a different subject. He started to talk about

Duroc

the crane incident on Gannet Gamma. He explained that nothing had been found to be wrong with the hoist brake on the crane. So why had the crane suddenly dropped a load and injured Gus MacIntosh? he asked. Initially this had seemed to be an incident without cause or reason. However, investigations into the other incidents that had occurred on both the GG and the dive vessel, MS *Merganser*, gave the investigators a clue. There was a common denominator between all the incidents.

Without explaining what he meant, Bluey had the meeting attendees on tenterhooks. He then told his audience that on the afternoon of the crane failure there had only been one qualified crane driver on GG. The relief driver had been due to arrive that evening. The qualified driver, whose name was Jim, who was not present at the meeting, had just finished offloading supplies from a supply vessel and had gone to the canteen for a break. So he had an alibi for that time. Bluey explained that it was still unclear who had been at the controls of the crane that afternoon, but one name had been identified as a possibility, that of a man by the name of Maclean. However, Maclean had left the GG the following morning and had never been seen or heard of again. Why would Maclean—or anyone else, for that matter—want to drop a crate of engineering parts and nearly kill someone? He or she must have had a pretty good reason.

"We have talked to Gus MacIntosh," Bluey continued. "He is OK, by the way, although he's not keen to work on GG any more. Gus tells us that just before the crate was dropped by the crane, he was looking at another crate that appeared to have been damaged. It was on the deck, and it intrigued him, although he has lost some of his memory since the accident and so he can't quite remember why he was looking at the damaged crate. Caitlin and I can only surmise what he saw. What we do know from our investigations is that the damaged crate is one of two that belonged to a contractor by the name of Scottish Pipeline Services. The crate had just arrived on the supply vessel, and by a process of elimination we know that this particular crate contained a pipeline pig, which was to be used in the USP1 pipeline the following day. Why would anyone be so desperate to stop someone from nosing around a broken crate containing a specialised piece of engineering equipment as to almost kill Gus MacIntosh? The answer is that if the pig contained something that the owner didn't want you to know about, then he might resort to desperate measures. The owner of the pig was so desperate, that once Ashe started to investigate what was going on, he attacked me whilst I was examining the crane hoist mechanism. Unfortunately for him, his unprovoked attack only resulted in a temporary injury, and I am still here to tell the tale today.

"You will see that as a result of our investigations we have found a consignment of around 25 kilos of drugs that were inside the pig. Who did the drugs belong to? There can only be one answer. There is one company whose name consistently comes up in relation to the drugs and who were around when there were attempts to prevent the pig being recovered."

Bluey looked down the long conference table, straight at Stylo, and said, "That company is Scottish Pipeline Services."

Caitlin thought she had never seen a man look so menacing. But Stylo stayed silent.

"SPS sourced the pig and launched it into the pipeline," Bluey said. "When the location of the pig was found, SPS managed to switch the radiographs that were taken in order to mislead Ashe into thinking that the pig was conventional. But you knew all along that it wasn't, didn't you, Stylo? We think that you arranged for one of your colleagues to find his way onto the dive team that was to take the radiographs. Unfortunately, that sortie didn't go to plan, not because of anything that Scottish

Duroc

Pipeline Services did, but because the engineers on the MS *Merganser* didn't do their safety checks thoroughly enough and one of your own team nearly died. Not only that, in order to get your man Bogie onto the radiographics team, you arranged for an old petrol head from Falkirk to organise an unfortunate road traffic accident. The result of that was that someone else nearly died—but you got Bogie into the diving bell!"

Stylo stared straight at Bluey, his grey eyes transmitting pure hate. But Bluey wasn't finished. He went on. "When it came to preparing for the pipeline by-pass around the pig, guess who got the job to install the stopples?" A young rookie engineer sitting halfway down the table and transfixed by the proceedings, mouthed, "Scottish Pipeline Services."

"Scottish Pipeline Services. Their sticky paw prints are all over this. Scottish Pipeline Services were the delivery team who made things happen, but not the people who were making the decisions. Unfortunately for them, they got greedy and started to stick their fingers in the till. You see, we have found that the pig wasn't intended to be carrying drugs. That was Stylo's idea. His boss had much grander plans for using the pigs as a means of transportation. However, when Stylo found that their almost undetectable illicit transport system was often operating below capacity, he decided to move in and fill up the empty space. This is why the pig was carrying the drug Monkeydust. It was a relatively low-value product, but a money spinner for Stylo." He looked again at Stylo. " I wonder what your Mr Big would have to say if he knew that you were skimming profits off his venture?" Bluey looked around the table. Clearly some of the people at the meeting were horrified. Jason Suínos from the GG was looking daggers at Stylo.

As for Stylo, he knew the game was up. He suddenly sprang up and made for the door. Martyn Southwick put his foot out and Stylo went sprawling onto the floor, scudding across the polished surface until his chin met the skirting board with a crunch.

Bluey was nothing if not thorough. He had anticipated that Stylo or someone else might try to do a runner. He had asked two of Scottish Police's best plainclothes detectives to be present. The brawny detectives sprang on Stylo. There was a short "click, click" as the handcuffs engaged, and in less than five seconds, whilst his rights were being read, Stylo's freedom came to a sudden end. The two detectives marched their suspect off to the awaiting squad car.

The room went quiet. The drama was over for now, and Bluey suggested that they take five minutes for a leg stretch, to give his audience some time to take things in and for a bit of gossip. As they filed out of the room, Caitlin turned to Bluey and asked, "But it wasn't all down to Stylo, was it?"

"No. We know that Stylo had a team of thugs working for him. The drug running was quite lucrative and so he could afford to have hired help. However, Stylo and his gang were just the leg-men. There were at least four of them. They included the man known as Maclean, who I suspect was responsible for the crane failure incident. He was just trying to stop people seeing what was inside the shattered crate from SPS, because we now know that it contained the pig that was carrying the merchandise. Then there was the man we know as Bogie, the petrol head from Falkirk who was responsible for the serious injury to the radiographer, and the "Unshaven One" who kidnapped you and was apprehended at the redundant Duroc tank. But there are undoubtedly more. I think it's highly likely that they also work for Scottish Pipeline Services. But the master-mind will be found elsewhere."

A few minutes later it was obvious that there had not been much gossip. As the meeting attendees returned to their seats around the long conference table, Caitlin noticed there were a

Duroc

lot of very pale faces. Was that guilt, or shock at what Bluey had revealed? You could have heard a pin drop. At the far end of the table, there was an unclaimed Rubik's cube. Caitlin couldn't work out who was the owner, although she had an idea.

Bluey was standing again at the end of the long conference table. "There were several things going on within the Duroc group of companies. Mr Reynolds admits that the insurance company suspected Duroc Petrochemicals of fraud. We now know that illicit merchandise was being imported into Scotland through the USP1 pipeline. As you heard before we took our short break, Stylo was at the heart of what has been going on," said Bluey. "But he was not the ring-leader. He was just taking advantage of the situation. Clearly, more than anyone else, Stylo had access to both the GG and also to Duroc Petrochemicals, in his role as an established and frequently used contractor. He was the perfect lieutenant for Mr Big, as he not only supplied and launched the pigs, but he was also a qualified diver. However, Ms Barland and I believe that the purpose of the pig runs was not to carry Monkeydust. That was just Stylo's sideline. The pigs *were* a transport system, but they were being used for something much more valuable." Bluey paused whilst he scanned the faces around the table. Seventeen pairs of eyes looked back at him. Were some faces sweating? Certainly, some of the younger faces were astonished. Was this inspector from Ashe suggesting that their employer was corrupt? If he was, it was the first they'd known about it.

"So, if the primary merchandise that the pig was carrying was not Monkeydust, what was it?" quizzed Bluey. No one volunteered a solution. "Our forensic scientist has identified another product contained within the body of the pig, and its value suggests that it is the reason why it was worth taking the risk of importing it via the pipeline. We have found that the pig removed from the pipeline contained, in addition to the Monkeydust, a quantity of gemstones. These stones were identified as red diamonds. Red diamonds are the fifth most valuable item by weight in the world. They are much more valuable than gold. The world's most valuable red diamond is known as the Moussaieff Red and is valued at around $20 million for a mere 5.11 carats." Bluey could tell the audience was impressed. He went on, "The only snag with red diamonds is that there are very few examples of them in existence. That's why they are so valuable. It seems that SPS's pig was carrying about five times the total world stock of red diamonds!"

From the back of the room someone called out, "How can that be?"

"We are still carrying out tests," said Bluey. "But the only way we can rationalise this, is that the diamonds on the pig are man-made, synthetic diamonds. There is a very specialised process called HPHT, or "High Pressure, High Temperature," whereby high-quality diamonds can be synthetically manufactured. The way it is done is that a small quantity of diamond 'seeds' are melted in a press at 1400 degrees centigrade and pressures of 870,000 pounds per square inch, along with a solvent metal. The solvent metal, made up of iron, cobalt and nickel, forms a flux which dissolves a graphite source and precipitates pure carbon onto the seed diamond. The growth time can vary from several days to weeks, depending on the size of the diamond being produced." He had their attention. A couple of young engineers were scribbling furiously in their notebooks, having just discovered their new career route to perpetual happiness!

Bluey went on, "The manufacturing process is actually irrelevant. It probably takes place in the Far East somewhere. High quality red diamonds, even if they are not natural ones, are still very, very valuable. What is important, is—who is smuggling these through your USP1 pipeline? Mr Stylo has very clearly

Duroc

demonstrated to us that Scottish Pipeline Services had a practical role to play in this illicit venture, but it is our opinion that the scheme was administered elsewhere."

Bluey paused for effect, and scanned the faces around the table. There was a group of innocent young faces—the recently recruited, newly qualified engineers and shift managers from both the petrochemicals plant and the rig. It was very unlikely that any of them had the experience or contacts to mastermind the illicit operations. Amongst the more senior people around the table, two men were looking particularly shifty. Brodric Reynolds and Jason Suínos were both staring at the table. Brodric was a strange puce colour. In fact, they were both very angry, but for different reasons.

"So, who had both the motive and the opportunity to put the diamonds in the pig?" continued Bluey. "We know that the practical stuff was done by technicians, mainly from Scottish Pipeline Services, and that they had an ancillary money-making scheme of their own, involving drugs. But none of them were the mastermind behind the operation. It is most likely that Mr Big was a manager somewhere within the Duroc businesses." He looked at the panicky faces of the young engineers around the table. They obviously thought that he was implicating them.

"We don't think that the junior management were involved. But there *was* a motive in Duroc Petrochemicals, because we know from the recent incidents there that it was a newly acquired business which was short of cash and didn't have enough money to pay for the supply of feedstock. So, who could be the guilty party? It had to be someone with business expertise, who also had links with Scottish Pipeline Services and both Duroc Petrochemicals and the GG. The pigging operation was managed from Gannet Gamma. The installation manager had to know whenever pigging operations were planned, but so did the engineers at each end of the pipeline." Bluey turned towards

Iain Talbot, the plant engineer at Duroc Petrochemicals. "What was your involvement in the pigging operations?"

Talbot replied, "We pig pipelines frequently. My main responsibility is for those pipes within the petrochemicals complex. I authorise all those jobs, but we undertake the pigging ourselves and do not use Scottish Pipeline Services." "The main raw materials pipeline pigging contract is placed by the installation manager on the rig. My only involvement with USP1 is to receive copies of the pigging information paperwork, such as pigging logs and the results of testing, for our records."

"But you knew that the pigging information was incomplete," said Caitlin. "Surely that suggested to you that something was not right?"

"I do know now. But I am extremely busy, so things like pigging information just get filed until there is a need to refer to them," replied Iain.

Bluey registered the comment about the role of the installation manager. He swung around and faced Jason Suínos. "Mr Suínos, you are the installation manager on the GG, is that correct?"

"Yes."

"With a name like Suínos, I assume that you are not English?"

"No, I come from the Alentejo region of Portugal, but I have been working in the UK offshore sector for 15 years."

"And in the Alentejo region of Portugal, can you tell us what the word 'suínos' means?"

"Yes, the literal translation would be 'hog' or 'pig'!" Jason smiled at the joke.

The significance of his reply was not lost on the young and innocent engineers around the table. They were obviously thinking, *Who else would head up a pigging scam, other than Mr Pig?*

Duroc

Bluey was obviously thinking the same. "Who on Gannet Gamma places the pigging contracts with Scottish Pipeline Services?"

"I do."

"And who decides on the frequency of the pigging runs?"

"Me."

"So you would be in the best position to decide when additional pig runs are required."

"It's decided by the GG Management Team, not just me."

"Would you decide on what type of pig is required for each pigging run?"

"No. I tell them what we need the pig to do, and then the Drifters decide what pig type to use."

"The Drifters?"

"Yes, that's what we call Scottish Pipeline Services on the rig."

"So, what type of pig would be required to transport diamonds or drugs?"

"No comment." Jason Suínos was starting to get rattled.

"Jason, do you know anyone called Carl Dunne? He used to work on the GG."

Jason screwed up his eyes whilst he thought. "Yes, he is a broad scot. A bit difficult to understand!"

"Carl told us that he remembered hearing your voice in a phone call, when he was told to inspect the bellows on the petrochemicals plant."

Reluctantly, Jason agreed. He had told Carl Dunne to do that. But he had had no part in the diamond smuggling.

"Carl also told us that he thought he recognised the voice as belonging to someone called Moura."

Jason looked puzzled.

"You see, we believe that the name Moura is an alias. We have also discovered what the word 'moura' means. Do you know what 'moura' means?"

"No idea."

Bluey looked at the young engineers, and someone speculated. "A pig?"

"Bang on!" said Bluey. "Moura is a breed of pig! Not only that, but can you guess where it comes from?"

By this stage everyone had given up the guessing game.

"Well, I'll tell you. It comes from a place in Brazil. In southern Brazil, actually. The name of the place is Duroc!" The room went completely quiet. "Now, Mr Suínos, or whatever your name is, tell me, is it my imagination, or doesn't someone whose name means a pig, and whose alias also means a pig, one that comes from a place that has the same name as your company, Duroc, doesn't that all sound a bit coincidental when we're here to talk about a pigging scam?"

Jason didn't know how to reply. It was getting late and the meeting was getting restless. Suddenly it was Brodric Reynolds who stood up and bluntly said to Bluey, "Scrimshaw. My office. Now!"

The meeting collapsed into disarray as Reynolds left the room followed by Bluey, Caitlin, Jason Suinos and another man in orange overalls.

They all followed Reynolds into a large office on the first floor of the administration building. Bluey and Caitlin entered the office first and Reynolds brusquely waved to two chairs. He was standing behind them when they heard a clicking sound. The sound of the door being locked by Suinos. Brodric walked around to his desk seat and looked sternly across at his two guests. "You are completely wrong," he said.

"About what?"

"About Jason and Moura."

Duroc

"Why?"

"My colleague Jason is definitely not Moura." There was a long pause. "I am"

Caitlin gasped.

"But now that you know, we have a bit of a problem. Because I can't let you go!"

Caitlin looked furious. Being kidnapped once had been bad enough, but twice was just beyond the pale. "What do you mean, you can't let us go?"

Before they knew what was happening, Bluey and Caitlin were both held down in their chairs whilst Moura went to work with reels of webbing tape. Despite Duroc's impoverished circumstances, it was obvious the one thing they were not short of was gaffa tape. First Moura taped their mouths and then he used long lengths to bind them both to their chairs. They were effectively immobilised. As Moura and his two henchmen left the room, Moura told Jason to unplug the telephone. The door clicked twice. Once to unlock, and again as it was relocked.

Bluey looked across at Caitlin. Her eyes looked scared. He needed to think fast. It had been about 4:30 p.m. when they had left the conference room. The day workers in the offices finished at about 5 p.m. It must be after that now. The offices would be becoming more and more deserted. It was also starting to get dark. Lights from under the door went out as the secretary's office closed down for the night. And then it was quiet, except for the rumble of the production plant outside the window. Nothing happened for some time. Bluey's eyes were closed, because neither he nor Caitlin could speak. Suddenly he heard a chair banging up and down. He opened his eyes to see Caitlin literally bouncing up and down on her chair to get his attention. She swivelled her eyes sideways in the direction of the door. There were flashes of yellow and orange light showing under the door. Then he noticed wisps of smoke. There was a fire outside.

Bluey suddenly realised what Moura had meant when he'd said, "I can't let you go." There was about to be another unplanned incident at Duroc Petrochemicals, and this one was destined to have two fatalities.

They didn't have much time. No time to fiddle about, trying to find ways of releasing each other from their bindings. By that time, they would both be cooked meat. Bluey looked around the office and in the half light, he noticed a safety device on the wall. He copied Caitlin's action and started bouncing up and down on his chair. With each bounce the chair moved about a centimetre across the floor. It was exhausting and noisy work. Would Moura hear him? Slowly the chair and its captive moved towards the wall. Just as he was nearly at the wall, the chair caught on some carpet edging and with the next bounce Bluey and the chair started to topple. He crashed to the floor and was completely immobile. The chair wouldn't move any further. As he lay considering his demise, he heard Caitlin starting to bounce on her chair. He was facing the wall, so he couldn't see her, but he could hear her getting closer. Lying on the floor he could see under the door. He could tell that the fire was also getting closer. It would be only a matter of time....

Caitlin wasn't sure why Bluey had suddenly started to bounce towards the wall. But one thing was certain, he couldn't go any further. She thought he might have been injured in the fall. As she approached him, one tiny bouncing step at a time, she could make out his eyes. He was now trying to tell her something. She looked around. What was he trying to tell her? She kept bouncing towards the wall. The smoke was now starting to enter the room and it was becoming difficult both to see and to breathe. Then she saw it. She knew exactly what she had to do.

Duroc

She had two metres to go, but she had to avoid making the same mistake that Bluey had made. She was their only chance. In mid bounce she threw herself sideways and the chair turned through 90 degrees. On and on she went, with the smoke getting thicker all the time. She was finding it more and more difficult to find her target. Still almost a metre to go. In a last desperate attempt, she flung her full weight backwards in the chair, and it started to topple. Would it make the target? She couldn't see behind her. The chair crashed against the wall and the back support crashed into the little glass-fronted red box on the wall. There was a quiet tinkle of breaking glass falling to the floor, followed by all hell breaking loose as the seven bells of the building fire alarm burst into life. Of course, there was no one there who needed to be evacuated other than the two occupants of Moura's by now rather warm office. Caitlin hoped the alarm was automatic, so that it would go straight through to the fire brigade.

Caitlin and Bluey were trussed up on the floor as the fire continued to spread. The good news was that by toppling their chairs they had inadvertently ended up with their noses on the floor, which was where the most oxygen was. The dense smoke swirled above them. The din of the fire alarm was still ringing in their heads, and then they heard it. The nee-naw of the fire engine sirens hurtling towards Duroc Petrochemicals.

*****

It was dark, but the lead fireman's helmet lamp cut a narrow shard of light into the swirling smoke. There was a hand on his shoulder. It was his colleague, following in his very footsteps. The only sounds were the rasping breathing of the BA sets and a report from the lead fireman about what he could feel around him. "Staircase—handrail on left." Communication was succinct—it used up air and limited airtime for other crew members. They plodded slowly forward, trailing a heavy hose reel up the concrete stairs. They had yet to find the source of the fire. At the top of the stairs, they reported their location and the fire status to the BA controller. In front of them was a set of twin closed fire doors. Through the vision panel in the doors, they could see brightly coloured tongues of flame flickering at the ceiling level. The fire was progressing through the suspended ceiling. The lead fireman turned and nodded to his colleague. He got the "thumbs up" and carefully eased one of the doors open to avoid a sudden ingress of oxygen into the opaque corridor beyond.

They moved steadily forward. A quick blast of water from the hose up to the ceiling quenched some of the dancing flames. They felt a door on their left. One of the firemen touched the door knob with the back of his hand. It was hot. They radioed back that there was a significant fire in the first office on the left. Both fire fighters crouched down. The leader carefully opened the door whilst his mate sprayed a fan of water into the room. Staying below the smoke, they checked for any sign of life. The office was empty and so they withdrew and closed the door again and reported their findings over the radio.

Next was the office on the right. Using the same procedure, they entered the small office. The office was like Hades and the fresh oxygen admitted through the door caused the fire to flare up even more. In the light of the inferno, the firemen could immediately see that there was no one in that office. They reported back to the BA Controller that they had found a major source of fire in the small office on the right. The controller looked at his plan of the building and told the firefighters that it was a secretary's office and that there was another, larger office beyond that which needed checking. There was a door in the opposite wall that was already well alight. A blast from the hose quenched the flames on the door, long enough for the other fireman to try the door handle. It was locked. Without hesitation, the fireman raised his boot and with a single kick the door fell backwards into the room. Fire was already progressing across the ceiling but the lower part of the room was smoke-logged. Some of the glass in the external window had shattered in the heat and was venting smoke to the outside. They crouched down again. The smoke was less dense at that level. The leading fireman saw the shape of a person lying on their side on the floor. They didn't know it then, but it was Caitlin and she was unconscious. "There's someone here... Christ, he's tied up!" exclaimed the strained voice over the BA radio. The lead fireman instantly recognised that the fire in the secretary's office was now too severe for them to get a casualty out that way. He called for back-up to bring a ladder to the external window. As he was speaking, he fell over another body on the floor. "There's another one!" he announced. They quickly cut the tape holding the casualties to their chairs, and lifted the prone bodies over to the window, just as they got the message to stand back, as the external ladder was in place and a third fireman was at the first-floor level and about to break more window glass with his axe. As the tumbling glass hit the floor, the ladder fireman was already passing a scoop rescue stretcher through the window aperture, so that the casualties could be safely lowered down to the ground. It was only at this stage that they realised that one of the casualties was a young female. The lead fireman radioed the controller to indicate that the two casualties had both been bound to chairs, and that the police should be informed. He closed the communication with a request to "make pumps three," indicating a need for additional fire engines to tackle the spreading fire in the office building.

Both Caitlin and Bluey were still unconscious when they arrived at the ambulance. Their vital signs were OK, but they had breathed in smoke. Ironically, the webbing tape that had been used to gag them had actually saved their lives by minimising the amount of smoke that entered their lungs. As they arrived in the hospital A&E department both the casualties were starting to come around.

Chapter 22

Both Caitlin and Bluey were kept in hospital overnight for observation, in different wards. At the nurses' station in Caitlin's ward, the sister took a message from Caitlin's dad, who was asking which ward she was in, and when she would be discharged. Without checking the caller's identity, the sister cheerfully provided the information to the anxious father. She went to Caitlin's bedside and gave her the message. Caitlin thought that was a bit odd. Her mum and dad had visited the night before and knew which ward she was in. However, she didn't give it much thought, as a rather uninspiring breakfast had arrived. Shortly afterwards the hospital consultants came round and Caitlin was declared fit and ready for discharge. Caitlin rang Bluey on her mobile but made no mention of the phone call to the sister. Bluey was also being discharged and suggested that they book a taxi together to go home. They should meet up at the hospital reception at 11 o'clock, he said. Bluey thought to himself that being in hospital was becoming a bit of a habit, and a big worry for Debbie and the boys. He took his Rubik's cube off the bedside unit to occupy the time and mindlessly aligned all the red squares.

At just before eleven, Bluey collected the meagre possessions that Debbie and the boys had brought in the night before and headed down to reception. When he got there Caitlin hadn't arrived yet, and so he found a bench by the door to wait.

Simon W. Pain

Caitlin thanked the nurses in her ward and walked towards the lifts, to head down to reception. She called the lift. As she waited, she had her mobile in her hand and was scanning for new emails. The lift light pinged to announce its arrival. The lift was large enough to take a bed down to other floors. Just as the doors were closing, a hand reached around them to keep them from closing and a gowned doctor in green scrubs and a surgical mask rushed into the lift. He turned away from Caitlin to face the panel of buttons and mumbled through his mask, "Reception?"

The voice sounded vaguely familiar, but Caitlin just replied, "Yes, please."

The doors of the lift rattled shut and the lift slowly started to descend at a sedate pace clearly designed not to alarm bed-bound patients. Suddenly the lift stopped. The doctor turned to face her, his arm raised in a threatening manner. Instinctively Caitlin shrieked and lashed out, swinging her heavy handbag and catching the doctor's cheek. His mask fell off and Moura's angry eyes stared back at her. Realising the threat, Caitlin defensively backed away until she hit the lift wall and could go no further. Moura sprang forward, nursing his stinging cheek. Then his hand came down to her neck and she felt a sharp prick as the needle entered her skin and injected 50 ccs of Monkey-dust into her vein.

Her mind was muddled. She still held the mobile phone in her left hand. On the back was an SOS button. She pressed it but felt consciousness slipping away. She needed to press the lift alarm. She weakly swung her arm at the lift control panel and bells started to ring. That was the last she heard as she slumped to the floor.

Bluey's phone jangled. He looked at the screen and it read "Caitlin—SOS." He immediately rang her back. He thought that he faintly heard a phone ringing in the direction of the lifts. But

Duroc

Caitlin didn't respond. Suddenly the bells on the outside of the lift started to ring, indicating some sort of a problem. The receptionist immediately left what she was doing and called security. "The lifts are stuck," she said into the phone.

In less than a minute, two blue-clad security officers came running into reception. One of them carried a jemmy bar. They glanced at the lift locator panels. The middle lift was stuck between the 2nd and 3rd floors. Bluey decided to follow. At the second-floor foyer the security men stopped and tried to jimmy open the middle lift doors. Bluey tried Caitlin's phone again. He could hear it ringing in the lift shaft.

One of the security men used the override key to switch the lift into manual operation whilst the other succeeded in prising open the lift shaft doors. He looked up the shaft and called to his mate that the lift was starting to move downwards. It had only taken a few minutes to get the lift back to the second-floor level. Bluey tried Caitlin's phone again. There was a ringing from inside the lift, but Caitlin wasn't answering. Why not?

As the security men prised open the inner lift doors at the second floor, they looked in. All they could see was Caitlin collapsed in a heap on the floor below the lift control buttons. There was no one else in the lift. They looked up and saw that the hatch in the ceiling of the lift was gaping open. Bluey shouted at the security men to get help for Caitlin, whilst he looked up through the open lift hatch. He could see steel cables and guide rails disappearing up into the darkness. He switched on the torchlight on his phone and held it up to the hatch. In the dim light he could see a green-clad figure almost at the top of the lift shaft, climbing up the steel lift guides.

The cavalry arrived in the foyer, with doctors, nurses and a gurney trolley. Caitlin stirred as she was carefully lifted onto the gurney. She saw Bluey, and just managed to mutter, "Moura," before she was whisked away by the medics. Bluey saw that she was in good hands, and so he jumped into the only remaining free and working lift and went to the top floor. The lift seemed to take forever as Bluey considered the meaning of what Caitlin had said. The only explanation was that the figure in the lift shaft had been Moura, and that he was in some way responsible for the attack on Caitlin. As the lift lumbered its weary way up to the top floor, Bluey phoned his police friend Jim Crieff and told him that there was an emergency on the roof of the hospital.

The lift clunked to a stop and the doors opened, as if in a theatre where someone was about to announce the start of a drama. Bluey looked around the bright foyer. It had a large lantern glass roof casting daylight in all directions. On the opposite wall, there was a single brown door that had the words "Roof Access—Maintenance permit required" stencilled on it. He tried the door, but it wouldn't open. No time for a permit, he thought. He stepped back and took a lunge at the door. He crunched against the door but it still didn't open. His shoulder hurt. As he rubbed the shoulder, he tried the door handle again. "What a dipstick!" he thought as the unlocked door swung open easily when pulled towards him! He stepped into a small enclosure with a metal staircase going upwards.

He stepped cautiously onto the metal treads, which creaked ominously as he applied his weight. At the top of the flight of steps there was a blue door with a panic bar. He carefully pressed the bar, releasing the door lock. The door opened slightly and Bluey slipped around the edge onto a flat roof. Immediately to his right was a box-like structure clad in corrugated steel. It looked like it housed the lift winding gear. It had a closed door on one side. As he watched, the handle of the door started to turn. Bluey ducked out of sight as Moura, still dressed in medical scrubs, stepped out of the winding house door. Moura crept furtively around the roof top, looking over the roof parapets at various places, as if he was looking for something. Bluey stepped into view. He wasn't going to use Moura's alias. "Looking for something, Reynolds?"

Moura swung around to confront him, his face furious. Then, without a word, he moved to the roof parapet, swinging one leg at a time over the top until he was facing out over the abyss. Bluey froze as Moura was about to jump. "Don't do it, Brodric!" he said quietly.

"It's all over for me," was the reply. And then, without any further word, Moura tumbled over the edge and disappeared from sight. Bluey's heart was in his mouth as he ran to the parapet and looked anxiously over the edge. Imagine his surprise when he found himself looking into Moura's face, no more than two metres down. Moura was lying on his back on the floor of a window cleaner's gondola. He sat up and pressed a button and the gondola started to descend. He grinned and lifted a hand in a half farewell wave to Bluey, laughing as he saw Bluey's astonishment.

The descent of the gondola was painfully slow as it had seven stories to travel before reaching ground level. Bluey searched all around the flat roof before he found the cable feeding the power to the gondola's motors. The cable was fed from a large grey socket plugged into the side of the lift winding gear housing. Bluey grabbed the socket with two hands and pulled it until it disconnected. He ran back and looked over the parapet. The gondola had dropped by about three floors but it had come to a halt. Moura was furious, but there was little that he could do. By this time, Jim Crieff and a squad of policemen had arrived on the roof. Bluey briefed Jim and they looked together over the edge at the raging Moura. He was starting to hammer on the windows of the hospital. Jim called for assistance from the fire brigade's aerial platform. Crieff left a couple of policemen at the roof level before he and Bluey went down to the 4th floor.

Simon W. Pain

At the 4th Floor, hospital patients were transfixed by the image of a doctor in green scrubs on the window-cleaning gondola raving outside their windows. He was hammering on the glass with his fists, but to no avail. Nurses were dashing about, trying to get their patients away from the windows, just in case the glass broke. Taking over from Bluey, Jim was trying to calm Moura down. He was having to shout through the double glazing, telling Moura that if he calmed down, they would re-connect the power to the gondola. Moura continued to rave. More police were arriving at the ground level of the hospital and sirens announced the arrival of the fire brigade's elevating platform.

One of the nurses who had been watching events out of the 4th floor windows spoke to Bluey. "I think that he has just injected himself," she said, referring to Moura. Certainly, Moura was not raving any longer; he was slumped at one end of the gondola. Jim spoke urgently into his radio. "Get that aerial platform up here!" he ordered. Hydraulics whirred on the platform and its elegant cranked arms started to open as two firemen were lifted up to the 4th floor. By the time the fire brigade's platform was alongside the gondola, Moura was unconscious. One of the firemen transferred across to the gondola and got the insensible Moura onto the aerial platform. By the time they reached the ground, there was a reception committee of uniformed policemen, doctors and nurses to take care of the unconscious Moura.

*****

Caitlin was starting to stir in her hospital bed, having been treated for a drug overdose. She looked across at the next bed and rubbed her eyes. She was seeing some men in black. Eventually, her thought processes caught up with her sight senses

Duroc

and she realized she was looking at two policemen. Why were there policemen in her ward? She looked at the figure in the next bed. It was her nemesis, Moura. Suddenly she was wide awake, all her senses bristling. One of the policemen looked across. "It's OK," he said, seeing her anxiety, "he's out of it and, in any case, when he wakes up, he'll be under arrest."

Caitlin was panicking. Here in the same room as her was the source of all her recent woes. He must also have been the one behind the incident at the helicopter escape training, and she didn't like it. Just then Bluey walked in. She threw her arms around his neck and pleaded with him to get her out of here. Bluey was also surprised to see Moura in the same small ward as Caitlin, although he realised the hospital staff knew none of the background. They just knew them both as drug overdose cases. Within five minutes, Caitlin's bed was being wheeled out into another, safer ward, but Caitlin never settled and four hours later she was on her way home.

Bluey also headed home. Moura was in custody and Jim Creiff and his team were searching for Suínos. It would only be a matter of time before he and the other gang members were found. After all, they all had links to Duroc.

THE END

ABOUT THE AUTHOR

SIMON WATSON PAIN is a Chartered Mechanical Engineer and is author of a series of technical books about health & safety. *Duroc* is his first venture into writing a novel. He is a has spent over 30 years working as a senior manager in the international Chemical and Steel Industries. Prior to retirement he spent over 20 years running his own business as a health & safety consultant, achieving "Best International H&S Consultancy" in 2017. He graduated from Birmingham University, with a post graduate diploma from the University of Loughborough. He is a Fellow of the Institute of Mechanical Engineers, a Fellow of the Energy Institute and a Member of the Institute of Occupational Safety & Health.

Simon lives in rural southwest Scotland with his wife Anne.

North Sea Wind Storm

By

James Boschert

A major drug deal is underway and loose ends are being taken care of when two things go wrong: two murders that were supposed to look like a suicide and an accident get noticed – one on an English railroad, and one on board an ocean-going barge.

As police are sent to investigate both seemingly unrelated incidents, the men at sea find themselves in dangerous waters. Who among them is on the take, and who is on the level? Who can be trusted when all of them are enduring the special man-made hell of life on an oil barge? As if deadly drug runners weren't enough to contend with, a convergence of storm winds and tides is creating the kind of waves that can make even the largest ships disappear without a trace...

Penmore Press
www.penmorepress.com

Better To Die
BY
Steve Smith

1996: Sergeant Nick Adair defends British Army border post "Hotel 55" from being overrun by the IRA, but the only witnesses to his bravery tell a different tale, with themselves as heroes and Adair castigated as a coward.

2021: After a five-year stint with the French Foreign Legion, Jack Adair is determined to have a career as a Sandhurst officer, preferably in his father's old regiment, the King's Royal Rangers. But the KRR considers itself elite, professionally and socially, with scant room for a rough diamond like Adair. Cadet Vyvyan Phillips is more the thing: younger son of General Philips, the decorated hero of the Hotel 55 incident. The General's reputation shines so brightly, it blinds everyone but Jack to Vyvyan's incompetence.

There is far more to the murky events connected to Hotel 55 but over time they have been either suppressed or ignored. The rivalry between Adair and Phillips extends beyond the confines of training and field command. Both take a keen interest in fellow officer Gemma Page, of Intel Corps. And then the battalion deploys to Gaziantep.

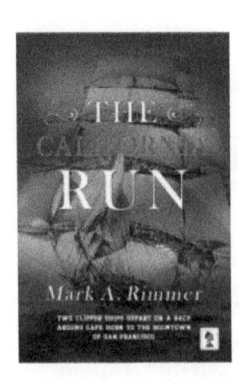

The California Run

by

Mark A. Rimmer

New York, 1850. Two clipper ships depart on a race around Cape Horn to the boomtown of San Francisco, where the first to arrive will gain the largest profits and also win a $50,000 wager for her owner.

Sapphire is a veteran ship with an experienced crew. Achilles is a new-build with a crimped, mostly unwilling crew. Inside Achilles' forecastle space reside an unruly gang of British sailors whose only goal is to reach the gold fields, a group of contrarily reluctant Swedish immigrants whose only desire is to return to New York and the luckless Englishman, Harry Jenkins, who has somehow managed to get himself crimped by the equally as deceitful Sarah Doyle, and must now spend the entire voyage working as a common sailor down in Achilles' forecastle while Sarah enjoys all the rich comforts of the aft passenger saloon.

Despite having such a clear advantage, Sapphire's owner has also placed a saboteur, Gideon, aboard Achilles with instructions to impede her in any way possible. Gideon sets to with enthusiasm and before she even reaches Cape Horn Achilles' chief mate and captain have both been murdered. Her inexperienced 2nd Mate, Nate Cooper, suddenly finds himself in command of Achilles and, with the help of the late captain's niece, Emma, who herself is the only experienced navigator remaining on board, they must somehow regain control over this diverse crew of misfits and encourage them onwards and around the Horn.

PENMORE PRESS
www.penmorepress.com

First Fleet

By

M Howard Morgan

Love, murder, betrayal, and adventure with the transportation of convicts from Britain in 1787 and the founding of the penal colony that became Australia.

With the American colonies closed to Britain the gaols overflowed and the criminal under-class posed a growing threat to the property-owning classes. A solution was required to deal with the overcrowded prisons. The answer lay in colonising the continent on the far side of the world – *Terra Australis Incognita*; the unknown continent.

Claimed for Britain by James Cook during his first voyage of discovery in April 1770, the government of the day launched an ambitious project; to make use of the criminal class to develop a new colony. Its aim to find a new source of trade and a establish a new base for Britain's Royal Navy to support the burgeoning empire. The First Fleet of eleven ships left Portsmouth in May 1787 tasked with those objectives. The First Fleet of convicts. The great experiment so nearly failed.

Jack Vizzard, a young and raw marine officer of affluent background, becomes a member of the expedition. Lawyer, newly commissioned subaltern and a murderer, Vizzard finds his acts of betrayal follow him to New Holland. But what awaits him there? Retribution and reconciliation? Or ignominy and death?

PENMORE PRESS
www.penmorepress.com

Penmore Press
Challenging, Intriguing, Adventurous, Historical and Imaginative

www.penmorepress.com